PURPLE YOUR PEOPLE

For access to lots of free stuff, register your book at www.purpleyourpeople.com using the code:

TRANSFORM ME

PURPLE YOUR PEOPLE

JANE SUNLEY

crimson

Published in Great Britain in 2011 by
Crimson Publishing, a division of Crimson Business Ltd
Westminster House
Kew Road
Richmond
Surrey
TW9 2ND

A catalogue record for this book is available from the British Library.

ISBN 978 1 78059 046 2

Typeset by RefineCatch Ltd, Bungay, Suffolk
Printed and bound by Ashford Colour Press, Gosport, Hants

ACKNOWLEDGEMENTS

To the multi-talented Purple People who are, at the time of writing: director Jo, who's been here from the start (what would I do without you?); co-director Helen, ethical, expert, energetic; Emily P, whose fine editing helped with this book; L & D and service guru MJ; Jonners, who came for a year and has so far stayed for seven; Sol, the custodian of talent toolbox™ who also attempts to teach us Spanish; Sally, always so dedicated and professional; Emily M, who, despite being the youngest, keeps us all in check; newbies Todd, Marina and Jax; kind and caring Ben; wacky yet professional Caroline; Jodi, who's just flown the nest but is still purple; and, of course, the fabulous Miss Fi. And finally to all our very talented associates and partners who allow a relatively small company to make a very big impact.

CONTENTS

1

The people stuff:
why it matters

Who wouldn't want and need their organisation to be as successful as possible? Put simply, nobody. We believe that business success is truly dependent upon three key 'I's:

1. **Ideas:** compelling innovations around which you can create an easily marketable brand.

2. **Investment:** capital for start-up and growth plus cashflow; the life-blood of every organisation.

3. **Individuals:** the right talented people, in the right roles, delivering innovations and high levels of service, working to their potential – in a happy and inspired way.

These three are of equal importance, yet the third 'I' is rarely given the attention, time, resources and investment it needs. There is a clear gap between recognising the power of people and delivering a robust people strategy in our fast-moving, ever more demanding and diverse world.

Becoming people-centric is the way to go

We love the courageous, determined and high-impact human resource director (HRD) who positions him/herself in a triangular relationship with the chief executive officer (CEO) and chief financial officer (CFO). This is the way to get things done, secure the necessary investment and create commitment from the top.

But this book is not just for organisations that are large enough to justify an HR resource. **Great people-centricity can still be achieved if you know how to make it joined-up and simple – that's what this book is all about.** One of our most successful SME (small and medium enterprise) clients, turning over in excess of £25m and winning many prestigious people awards along the way, has no internal HR resource at all.

Why does the people stuff, despite the best intentions, fall by the wayside so often? Because many business leaders and owners are often so busy dealing with the day-to-day stuff and fighting to survive and thrive that the subject of people just falls off the bottom of the list. Consequently people drop in and out of the organisation at an alarming rate, costing time, hassle and money. Most organisations don't measure the cost of replacing a leaver – it's just too difficult, too scary or both.

For a start there are the direct costs of recruiting a replacement, such as recruitment fees, time, interim cover, induction and so forth. The big impact, though, is made by the indirect costs – the expenditure people often don't even pause to consider.

These include:

- Knowledge loss
- General instability
- Service disruption/quality
- Customer relationships/loss
- Increased threat of competition
- People leaving as a result
- Drop in productivity
- Effect on morale
- Disruption to team dynamics
- Effects on reputation

You can probably come up with some more if you really think about it . . .

There's a great (true) story about a managing director who pitched the idea of recruiting a global HRD, for the first time, to his board of directors, only to discover they thought they already had one! This shows that (a) the board weren't giving much boardroom time to the third 'I' and (b) the expectations of said HRD must have been pretty low. We heard this from the person who was ultimately appointed to the role and then went on to take the organisation by storm. The board certainly knows it has a group HRD now.

So why isn't everyone doing something about it?

The answer is not earth-shattering. Put simply, growth organisations and their leaders lack the time and resources to actually deliver on the people stuff. It's not that they don't know it's important.

To prove what we've identified over the last 10 years, we asked an exclusive panel of over 40 leaders taken from our 'Purple Revolutionaries' and networks associated with Cranfield Business School and Lancaster Management University for their feedback. Here are a few of the outcomes:

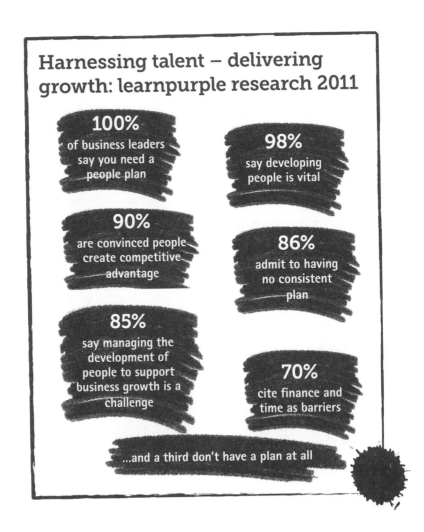

Harnessing talent – delivering growth: learnpurple research 2011

100% of business leaders say you need a people plan

98% say developing people is vital

90% are convinced people create competitive advantage

86% admit to having no consistent plan

85% say managing the development of people to support business growth is a challenge

70% cite finance and time as barriers

...and a third don't have a plan at all

While it's great that so many organisations recognise that getting the 'people stuff' right is the key to achieving objectives, there is clearly a gap when it comes to harnessing the power of individuals to help deliver business success and growth. In the majority of cases, it just isn't happening when it comes to putting in place a plan to support company milestones.

And that is what this book is all about.

Read it, refer to it, think about it, scribble on it, share it, steal the ideas in it — but above all, make it happen.

For the organisations that succeed in this, and they are the ones at the top of the 'fastest growing' or 'most successful organisation' lists, making super-profits as they go, they strive to be strong in all of the areas covered in this book.

So while becoming people-centric can't and won't happen overnight, welcome to the start of your journey. By breaking the important stuff down into manageable chunks it really is possible to achieve and definitely worth the effort – as you become more focused on your people and their development you will, no doubt about it, reap the benefits of an inspired, developing workforce that has the skills and personalities to progress the organisation further and achieve greater (and ever greater) business success.

2

Visions, missions, values and all of that

Visions, missions and values are simply what your organisation stands for. Although it's unnecessary to label them, for the record, quick and easy definitions are:

Vision: what the organisation aspires to be.

Mission: what the purpose of the organisation is.

Values: important shared beliefs and ideals that define organisational culture.

We're not in favour of long mission and/or vision statements that no one, not even the CEO, can remember. You'd be surprised at the number of well-respected companies that put 100 words on a brushed stainless steel plaque in their reception area and then hope everyone 'gets it'.

It's really essential that every single team member and potential team member can easily understand what you're all about; what you stand for; and where you're going.

Most important, this message needs to be consistent throughout the organisation.

Abercrombie and Fitch: funky, hip and trendy, but at the time of writing uses too lengthy a statement (see overleaf). Impossible for everyone to remember and therefore, in our view, impractical when it comes to getting everyone living the message.

Could anyone remember this?

Abercrombie and Fitch

'Abercrombie and Fitch desires to attract and retain the best available executive and key management associates for itself and its subsidiaries and to encourage the highest level of performance by such associates in order to serve the best interests of the company and its stockholders. The plan is expected to contribute to the attainment of these objectives by offering eligible associates the opportunity to acquire stock ownership interests in the company, and other rights with respect to stock of the company, and to thereby provide them with incentives to put forth maximum efforts for the success of the company and its subsidiaries.

'The A&F brand is more authentic and relevant than ever. The brand is our lifestyle, our focus—it ensures growth and promises stability. A great brand is a center of growth and revenue—it represents a relationship with customers. It's not a faddish chip to be cashed in on shortsighted gains. The value of having a great brand is far-reaching and cannot be overstated—it's a snowball effect. The A&F label gives us the ability to evolve, creating endless growth opportunities. It helps us attract the brightest, most talented young people from around the country. It attracts millions to our website. It allows for greater profit margins. It lessens the risk of moving on new business concepts. It promotes innovation. It ensures long-term profitability. It adds built-in value to everything we produce. It accelerates growth. It stabilizes. It gives focus and direction. It produces an emotional response in consumers. Overall, Abercrombie and Fitch focus upon high-quality merchandise that complements the casual classic American lifestyle.'

Google and Facebook do it more succinctly:

Google: *'To organize the world's information and make it universally accessible and useful.'*

*'**Facebook's** mission is to give people the power to share and make the world more open and connected.'*

A couple of decades ago, Fuji Film Corporation's unwritten, highly successful mission statement was alleged to be: 'Kill Kodak'.

But you can go one better and find the single, most perfect word for your business – after all, no one can forget one word.

Learnpurple's mission and vision statement is simply:

Transformation

Transforming for the better ourselves, our own business, our customers and clients, our partners and everyone we come into contact with.

Values

When it comes to values they have to be memorable and, vitally, **leaders (at all levels) must live those values every day and never (ever) compromise them.**

If you haven't yet defined your values it's important to do this properly and inclusively. This is a time when investment in an external facilitator is money well spent. Involve people rather than taking a top-down approach in isolation.

Once you start using your values to underpin everything you do, talk about them on a daily basis so they become memorable.

Until you're at that stage, however, you could, as some people do, put your values on posters or credit card-sized reminders – which is a start. In our view, though, it is far better to find a way to make sure people actually remember them, relate to them, like them and feel proud – that way they can truly live them every day.

Talk about your values all the time.

We like using mnemonics and acronyms because they make it easier for people to remember ideas.

Going through what you're about at interview stage and reaffirming during induction and beyond ensures that new people know exactly what to expect – it's also really motivating. Ask them from the beginning, **'Can you fully commit to these values?'**. If they can't, unless there's a very good reason for employing that person, don't take them on. It's unusual that someone can thrive and survive if they don't 'get' what you're

learnpurple's values:

AFFIRM IT

Achievement

Freedom (within a framework)

Fun

Image

Relationships

Make it simple

Improvement with originality

Trust and integrity

Virgin's values

- Value for money
- Quality
- Innovation
- Fun
- Competitive challenge

At the time of writing, Virgin operates to a 'brand cube' incorporating the wellbeing and happiness of its people and the sustainability of the planet with its values.

about. This is particularly true of organisations where people can make or break the brand.

Then, you need to remind continuously. Feed your values every day by referencing them in the decisions you take and throughout the way you operate.

You should also review your values annually, perhaps at your company meeting or conference, as it's important to make sure they are still absolutely relevant and true for your organisation.

If you only do three things:

1 Keep it simple and memorable

2 Leaders and champions must live the message – always

3 Feed your values daily to keep them alive

3

Reputation:
making yours great

This could be a very short chapter:

Q: How do you create a reputation as a great employer?

A: Become a great place to work.

That's easier said than done, though! Thankfully this is what this book of purple-ing your people is all about.

To deliver and strengthen a brand reputation through your people (and, let's face it, who doesn't want to do this?), it's necessary to attract the best people into your organisation. These are people who 'get' what you do, what you stand for, and are already sold (at least in part) on contributing to your success.

We firmly believe that as much thought should go into managing your reputation as an employer as it does into your marketing products and services.

If you come up with a new product you'll spend lots of time and resources making sure people know about it and understand what it can do for them. This creates the desire to buy. Most organisations are very good at this; however, relatively few are experts at positioning themselves as a best place to work. If you place the same importance on creating and managing your reputation as an employer as you do on the products and services you offer, the results will be very powerful.

Pre-internet times, it wasn't so damaging if employee reality didn't match the hype because it was pretty difficult for a potential candidate to know. Organisations were more or less on a level playing field; interviewees would make their decision about where they'd like to work from their experience at interview stage combined with the little information that was out there. And of course in those days people were a little more likely to do as their prospective employer told them (see Chapter 20 for information on generational disparities).

Fast forward to the internet years and candidates now have a wealth of information about an employer at their fingertips. It's now very easy to find out in a matter of seconds what the reality is behind the shiny veneer of what you say you are and do as an employer. Let's call this your people promise; this covers everything to do with the employee's experience as a part of the organisation. It encapsulates mission, values, leadership, culture, benefits, progression and other variables.

> The formal term for the people promise is the EVP or employee value proposition but I wouldn't want to put you off with too much 'corporate speak'.

It's not necessarily about investing in lots of resource. It's all about developing a clearly defined people promise which, when delivered consistently, will help an organisation to attract, engage and retain the best talent who are highly motivated and productive.

Lexington

Lexington (www.lexingtoncatering.com) is a lovely business that places a very high emphasis on delivering a strong offer to its people. It's punched above its weight and become not only an Investors In People Gold Standard employer (www.investorsinpeople.co.uk), but in 2011 also appeared at number 11 in the Sunday Times listing of the 'Top 100 Best Places To Work in the UK' with a top rating of three stars.

Its CEO had spent some time interviewing the shortlisted candidates for the year's graduate programme and was, in his words, 'surprised and blown away by their opinions of Lexington as an employer'. Many of them told him they'd applied solely because of Lexington's reputation in the marketplace as a fantastic place to work and progress. Lexington defined its values on day one and makes a big effort to live them through induction, development sessions but most of all by walking the talk – everyday.

And the really exciting thing is that once you understand the importance of a well-defined people promise, and are able to articulate it to the organisation and deliver on it, you will have created significant competitive advantage. What's not to love?

You need to make your organisation a great place to work and shout about it. Only then will your promise shine and the best talent come flocking.

But this cannot be a low-level project. It has to feed through the entire organisation, starting from the top; the owner, board, the CEO or MD. And it is not just an HR 'initiative'. It is a way of life to be built upon, refined, updated, cosseted, loved and cherished. That doesn't mean that the smart HRD couldn't sell in the idea and make it happen.

Purchasing decisions nowadays are made largely on the recommendation of a real person. That's why so many TV and media advertisements contain endorsements from celebrities or 'ordinary people'.

In a matter of seconds an individual can ask their 50, 500, 5,000 contacts on Facebook or Twitter what they think and feel about something. The same goes for prospective employees. So listen up:

If your organisation is not a great place to work, people will know.

As this book helps all types of company, including SMEs that might not employ an HR resource, here's our guide to constructing your shiny people promise.

First things first, you have to make this simple (a value which we at learnpurple believe everything should be) otherwise it won't get done.

In brief

What you can do to shape your people promise:

- Write down everything you offer now

- Consult your people about what they think and how well you deliver

- Ask them what could make it better

- Treat your people as individuals, so introduce a flexible approach to benefits

- Work out a people offer that fits the bill

- Write it down

- Communicate it

- Deliver it

Things you could include:

- The way people are led and managed

- How communication works

- How things are done around here (see Chapter 2 on values)

- Commitment to development and employee progression

- Recognition

- Reward

- Corporate social responsibility (CSR)

And so on. A well-crafted people promise will take the heat off compensation as the main motivator.

Here's a very simple structure for managing the consultation and shaping your people promise:

1. What do we offer our people that we are totally proud of as an employer?

2. What things are we OK at but could be better?

3. What things make us cringe?

If you're stuck for areas to consider, you could refer to the wheel in Chapter 23. Or use the chapters of this book as your guide.

Next, use this information to draw up a list of:

1. Things we should keep doing/do more of

2. Things we should stop doing/do less of

3. Things we should start doing

I can imagine your list is looking pretty daunting, but remember, all the planning in the world is worth absolutely nothing unless you do something with it. So divide your list into more manageable chunks or, better still, get your people to do the action planning (you may have to agree some ground rules).

Work out:

1. Quick wins: easy, fast and probably fun to do, requiring little resource

2. Easy to do but take more time and a bit more resource

3. Big, scary but necessary tasks which require resource and planning

> Remember, your people promise may well be a work in progress that evolves as you go along.

Then take three quick wins and make them happen. This should give you the momentum to carry on and tackle the rest. Rome wasn't built in a day, so make a plan and take it a step at a time. If you don't really know how to do it: **Stop.** Get help. Find a business you admire and ask someone there to mentor you or pay some people like us to come and support you.

Put some simple measures in place so that you can do a before and after comparison. When you can clearly see the value you are adding, it will keep you motivated (and persuade the doubters) to carry on.

Remember always that if you wouldn't be comfortable with the way you lead and deal with your people being reported on the front page of *The Times* (or imagine yourself on a 'back to the floor' reality show on TV), you are right to be making some changes.

If you only do three things:

1 Put some real effort into managing your reputation as an employer

2 Refine and deliver a great promise to your people

3 Take things a step at a time and look for the quick wins first to trigger momentum

4

Becoming a
people magnet:
attracting talent that fits

Being a great place to work and enjoying an outstanding reputation in the jobs market goes a long way when organisations are trying to attract the talented people they need to grow and prosper.

Your end goal

You continuously receive unsolicited applications from really talented people because they want to work for you.

And this will begin to happen as your reputation as a great place to work increases.

But, in the meantime, how do you attract talented people while saving time and money?

Before you do anything, stop right there and ask:

- Do we still need this role: what value does it add? (measure the role's outputs to decide)

- If there were a recruitment ban, what would we do to cover the work?

If you then decide you do need to recruit, follow these easy steps:

1. **Write a clear job description:** you'd be surprised how many people don't bother to do this. Everyone needs to be clear about what that person is actually there to do. Be straightforward and uncomplicated; here's a simple example:

Job description

Role: Superhero
Reports to: Chief superhero
Responsible for: Assistant superheroes, graduate trainee hero
Key objective(s):   Save the world

Key responsibilities:

● Protect the public at all times using superpowers for the good of humankind

● Maintain secret identity, always transforming in private

● Police day-to-day crime while also combating threats against humanity

● Risk own safety in the service of good without expectation of reward

● Maintain secret identity to protect friends and family

● Rid the world of super-villains and ensure criminals are brought to justice

● Manage own workload in order to maximise opportunities to do good

● Lead, develop and inspire team to give their best

You get the picture . . .

For more complex roles split the responsibilities into sections, e.g. operations, finance, sales, leadership and so on.

2. **Make an 'ideal' list:** write down the skills, knowledge, experience and attributes the ideal candidate will have. Better

still, get your team to do it. Some people think this is unnecessary and don't bother, but it's an easy way to make sure that everyone involved agrees on what's actually required. It will also help to plan the application process and interview questions. Here's a quick example:

Superhero: skills, knowledge, experience and attributes

	Must have	Nice to have
At least one extraordinary or superhuman power	✓	
Strong moral code, willing to risk own safety to protect others	✓	
Reluctance to kill or wield lethal weapons	✓	
Secret identity and own costume		✓
Own logo		✓
Experience of overcoming evil	✓	
Wide knowledge of super-villains		✓
Able to work independently as well as within a team	✓	
Proven leadership capability	✓	
Highly developed communication skills	✓	
Prepared to travel worldwide	✓	

And so on ... Again, you could put these into categories, e.g. skills, knowledge, experience and attributes. Make sure you specify what you really need, e.g. does someone really need five years' experience if they can prove they can do the job?

3. **Write your job advert:** once you are happy with what you need.Busy employers can't be doing with trawling through pages and pages of waffly CVs, so simplify the application process. Ask for:

- A one-page CV

- 10 bullet points as to why the applicant is perfect for the role

If applicants can't be bothered to follow instructions, condense their CV or take the time to write really good bullets, you can immediately sift them out of the process. (In our experience this applies to about 80% of applications and it really cuts down the work.)

The bullet points are very telling and will begin to give you an idea of whether a candidate 'gets' you as an organisation and would thrive within your environment. **Also, people who can write tend to be able to think clearly, logically and communicate well.** They also impress through the written word when they get into the role – very important when most things written today can potentially be seen by millions of people.

Your advert should reflect your values. Below is one of ours. You'll notice we are really selling our business to potential applicants and letting them know this is a partnership approach, i.e. what we can do for them:

Marketing Manager: join the purple revolution

learnpurple is a gift for any marketing professional. Over the past 10 years we've created one of the most innovative and exciting brands in the service industry support field. Through a series of creative and original products and services, we help other cool brands to engage, develop and retain the talent they need to grow.

This is a new position for us and, potentially, a real one-in-a-million opportunity for you.

We're all about maximising people potential, so here's the deal:

- We'll give you freedom (within a framework); an exciting challenge and a chance to shine

---

- You'll help us to market and grow the brand

- We'll teach you about business, people and other important stuff

- You'll progress and grow with the business

- We'll benefit from your considerable talents

- You'll be special: flexible, positive, self-sufficient and enthusiastic

- You're also likely to be a graduate looking for your second role in an environment where you can shine.

Email 10 bullet point reasons why you're the one, plus a one-page CV (including expected salary details) to emily@learnpurple.com. www.learnpurple.com

4. **Advertise internally:** make sure all vacancies are first advertised internally and never decide for people whether they should apply. (Read Chapter 13 for information on succession planning because, ideally, in most cases you'll already have the right applicant waiting in the wings.)

5. **Use your networks:** should you need to look externally. As an example:

For graduates:

- I'm a visiting fellow at two universities and also part of an excellent student mentoring network. This helps provide a steady stream of enthusiastic applicants to learnpurple. So volunteer for things – giving back often comes full circle and repays tenfold. You'll learn a lot from Generation Y (see Chapter 20) too.

- Consider taking students on sandwich courses for their year work placement – they generally like to return when they graduate and you'll have an enthusiastic, ready-trained candidate.

- We've also won awards for our student work placement provision, which brings us lots of applications from graduates. So if you do something similar, why not enter your scheme for an award. And remember, if you win, shout about it!

In general:

- Use online and other networks to spread the word that you are looking and send your job advert to everyone you can think of.

- If this doesn't work, resort to conventional means – using a recruitment agency, or advertising your job on a job board or in a magazine specifically for your industry.

If you only do three things:

1 Define what you actually need

2 Use the one-page CV and 10 bullets approach

3 Keep it fair and look internally first

5

Selection:
choosing the right talent for your business

This chapter is all about successfully choosing the right people to work with you. It's a little longer than some of the others because unless you recruit the right talent in the first place, it's an uphill battle to engage and retain them.

Having attracted a good selection of applicants, you'll need to shortlist those who are the most talented and best suited to the role and your organisation. If you've followed the advice in Chapter 4, the 10 bullet points provided by the candidate will be very useful in this task.

A real-life scenario

(names have been changed)

Gerry: 'So, Steve, how many applicants did you receive for the COO [chief operating officer] position?'

Steve: '229 – amazing, isn't it?!'

Gerry [to the rest of the meeting]: 'So do we know anyone on this list? That should help sift them a bit.'

Participants of the meeting proceed to read through the very long list of candidates shouting out their comments when they come across one they vaguely know . . .

It's great to use your network to identify possible candidates. However, it's important not to let this limit you in your choice – it's not fair or good for diversity and it's important to have a selection of candidates to compare.

A shortcut would be to use a good recruitment consultancy or headhunter to save time in the sifting process, though that depends on your budget.

However, if you decide to go it alone, make sure your recruitment advert is very specific otherwise you may well be faced with a large number of applications to sort through, many of whom won't fit.

Chapter 5

You can of course delegate the sift, as I always do, to a bright, focused and detail-oriented person. As long as the person doing the sifting is carefully briefed and works to clear criteria, this gives the candidate a fairer chance than they would have from a busy leader trying to fit it in. Having discussed this with many organisations, this business-critical undertaking seldom receives the attention it deserves because, unless you have the luxury of an HR department, the wrong people usually give themselves this task.

Once you've gone to the effort of advertising a job role publicly, everyone deserves an equal chance. In the case of Steve, he should have written his job advert more specifically, or perhaps this was simply an irresistible job opportunity. What I do know is that he didn't follow the 10 bullet point rule. So what happened next?

Steve sifted the candidates on a fair basis and was still left with 63. At this stage we'd recommend setting the candidates a written task, such as constructing those bullets, critiquing your website or some other work-related piece of writing. Some organisations use psychometric testing to sift. However, unless this is firmly embedded throughout the organisation, use it later on (see page 31).

Sifting tip

At the Purple Palace we love people who can write. Not only is this a useful skill, good writers can generally think clearly and logically and are skilled influencers. If the application you receive is poorly constructed and full of typos – think again!

When you invite candidates to interview, always let the unsuccessful ones know. Thank them for applying, offer them feedback and wish them well – if you don't bother it gives out a very negative message about your company. Few people call in for feedback but in the spirit of transformation we like to offer help towards self-improvement if they take us up on it.

The fab five of interviewing

Love it or hate it, a well-planned, structured interview can be a thing of beauty. Our fab five tips are:

Selection: choosing the right talent

1. **Write some standard questions** using your job description, person details, and culture of the organisation plus any other relevant factors. This way you are being fair to all and won't miss anything out. To help, we've included, on our dedicated 'Purple Your People' website, www.purpleyourpeople. com, a handy list of questions we have used in interviews (see page 175 for more details).

2. **Plan an outline structure**, e.g.:

● Rapport building

● Ask applicant to talk about him/ herself

● Ask questions from a list. Very important: listen very carefully and probe the responses before moving on – this is how you get to a deeper level and really begin to understand the candidate

● Discuss the role and the company

● Give the applicant an opportunity to ask questions

● Explain the next steps and stick to them – remember the under-promise over-deliver rule (see Chapter 9)

3. **Allow sufficient time.** For most roles you'll need to allow 40–60 minutes per interview. This person is potentially going to have a huge

Who interviews?

First interviews at the Purple Palace are usually done by a manager and a team member, since they know the job best. Directors are involved at the second stage. And, if appropriate, we like to invite the final shortlisted candidates in to work with his or her prospective colleagues. It gives both parties an opportunity to try each other out.

Useful cliché

You have two ears and one mouth, so use them in that proportion and resist overselling the company or role.

impact on your business – positive or negative – so it's worth taking the time to explore.

Questioning techniques

- Ask clear, unambiguous questions: 'There's a gap on your CV, what did you do between 2008 and 2010?'

- Ask open questions: 'Tell me about . . .'; 'How did you . . .'; 'What was the outcome?'

- Ask situational questions: 'Tell me about the last time you had to do a U-turn on one of your decisions'; 'What action would you take if your labour turnover began to increase?'

- Avoid closed questions, i.e. those requiring a 'yes' or 'no' response.

- Avoid leading questions: 'So you were successful at sales, then?'

- And if you get stuck or feel you aren't getting to the bottom of something, ask a 'Columbo question' – a dumb question that will allow further probing in a non-confrontational way: 'I might be missing the point here, so could you just explain exactly how you increased sales during the downturn?'

4. **Start to introduce information about your values** and 'the way we do things around here' (see Chapter 2). This is how you can start employee engagement activity, since it's a continuous and never-ending undertaking. If they join, you're ahead of the game. If they don't, they'll leave with a good impression and might even tell others what a great place to work you have.

5. **Write some notes.** Your goal is to decide whether the candidate should progress to the next stage of the selection process. It's vital to take notes so that you can (a) remember all

the important details and (b) provide a good brief for the second interview team. You could have this on an iPad or laptop and if more than one person is interviewing, one of the panel could take notes (ask the candidate's permission first – they never say no – it's polite and shows your respect and care).

Second interviews

For senior roles you might want to use a selection of techniques to test the candidate's attitude, skills and knowledge, based on the criteria in your job description and person requirements. For example:

● Business exercises – oral and written

● Presentations

● Group and individual challenges

● Psychometrics

● In-depth interviewing

If you don't have internal resources this is a challenge, so bring in the experts if you want to go to these lengths.

At the Purple Palace our second interview questions always include those based on the outcomes of an online psychometric test. The candidate can complete this in advance of the interview, which allows for preparation time. You should choose three or four key criteria which you want to find within the test results. For example, ours are:

● Goal focus

● Achievement focus

● Compliance

> In our 10-year history we have ignored the psychometric results three times and each time it's been very much to our detriment.

In our view psychometric tests should never be used for sifting purposes but only ever to shape the second interview and allow an in-depth look at the shortlisted candidates.

We strongly believe you'd have to be mad not to include psychometrics in any selection above the level of supervisor.

At second interview you should be able to have an adult-to-adult, two-way conversation with the candidate. The idea is to be really open and make them feel comfortable, ask the right questions, listen and probe properly. You might even find that you get to the stage where one or two openly admit during the interview that this isn't the right role for them.

In some instances, you might need to progress to third interview or other assessment activity, but we would recommend that you don't hang around too long: anyone worth their salt will have been snapped up by a more decisive company.

Once you've found your preferred candidate (or maybe a shortlist of two), consider whether you want to offer them a short time working within the business before the job offer is made. People will often take a day's holiday to do this – which is slightly naughty, though in our experience well worth the effort for both parties.

Hurrah! You've found your ideal person! Now call them up and make an offer – that's always the best bit! Then get a confirmation out straight away – you mean business!

We always say that if we're not jumping up and down with excitement at the prospect of a candidate joining, we don't make the job offer (again, the few times we've ignored our own rule we've always regretted it).

Citizen M hotels

Citizen M hotels is a very cool hotel brand. Among many awards and accolades, the company was voted Trendiest Hotel in the World on Trip Advisor in 2010 and 2011. At the time of writing Citizen M has properties in Scotland and Amsterdam and has secured several sites in London and New York. It has a novel way to recruit the right people. In a nutshell, it goes like this:

- *Three months before a property opens, it advertises a variety of available positions.*

- *The company invites 50–60 people in for four and a half hours on a Saturday morning (as you can imagine, this is a form of sifting in itself as only those who really want to be there turn up).*

- *Citizen M are looking for fun people who want to be themselves and give great service. Tattoos? Piercings? Green hair? Anything goes as long as the really important attributes are there.*

- *To test this, these 50–60 undergo a variety of activities:*

  ○ *For the first 45 minutes they have coffee and cakes and just chat and get to know each other (they're observed, obviously, to measure social skills).*

  ○ *Then they work in teams of four to make a collage by cutting pictures out of magazines and in their teams present their masterpiece at the end (this tests teamwork, confidence, creativity and presentation).*

  ○ *Next they work in pairs (again observed) and work together on a blindfold food tasting (this isn't really about their culinary prowess and palate but more to do with trust, relationships and working in partnership).*

○ Finally they work in groups and talk about who their heroes are and why. (This is about the ability to share feelings and it says a lot about character, sincerity and judgment.)

○ The selection is made and, since it's a while until the property opens, the successful candidates are invited back for a party (good 'engagement points' there; they will already know one another pretty well and have a good grasp of the organisational values before they start).

Big tick, Citizen M!

If you only do three things:

1 Sift fairly, giving it the time it deserves (or delegate to someone who can)

2 Prepare properly and structure your interview

3 Ask great questions, listen and probe

6

The Big E:
the whys and hows of
employee engagement
and why it starts here

Chapter 6

A lot of people are put off by corporate-sounding terms like 'employee engagement', so let's call it **'The Big E'** to make it more welcoming! Whether you employ five or five hundred thousand people, The Big E is going to have a very big effect on your business performance.

It's a fact that if your employees are engaged they will be more productive and more likely to stay with you, thrive and progress – therefore they will deliver a better brand, business and results.

So what's engagement all about? We like this definition from Wikipedia:

> 'An engaged employee is one who is fully involved in and enthusiastic about his or her work and thus will act in a way that will further the organisation's interests.'

In our view, The Big E:

- Goes beyond motivation and job satisfaction

- Cannot be requested or demanded as part of the role

- Is a state of mind whereby employer and employee understand and honour their commitments to one another

According to a 2011 Confederation of British Industry (CBI) trends survey, seven out of 10 employers consider improving employee engagement as the priority.

- Is brought about by the employee's desire to act in the best interests of work and colleagues

- Which in turn is brought about by delivery of the people offer (see Chapter 3)

Good employers have always been doing the right things to engage their people – even if they've never heard of the term 'employee engagement'. Having willing, enthusiastic and committed people simply makes good business sense.

At learnpurple we measure engagement by degrees of **purpleness**. A fully purple – thus engaged – person is completely committed and willing to act in the best interests of the business and fully support their colleagues. Metaphorically speaking, if you were to slice one in half across the middle, like a stick of Blackpool rock, they'd have 'learnpurple' written all the way through. You don't have to revert to Crippen-esque practices to test engagement, though. All you need to do is ask the right questions; and we have a wonderful engagement indicator survey on our website with questions like these in it! (See www.purpleyourpeople.com – free for 100 people or less.)

Scary statistic

Typically only about 20% of a workforce will be fully engaged, about 20% will be disengaged and the rest could go either way.

Sources: Blessing White, Corporate Leadership Council, Gallup, learnpurple

You have to keep on checking engagement, though. We check informally as appropriate and also formally as part of our review process. We ask, 'On a scale of one to 10, how purple are you?' This provides a good basis for discussion during the one-to-one ('What would make you a 10?'). It also allows for a quick and easy measure of our overall purpleness as an organisation.

'Always Be Collecting Dots'

In his excellent book Setting The Table, *charismatic New York restaurateur (and purple friend) Danny Meyer writes of his 'ABCD' policy. This stands for* **'Always Be Collecting Dots'**, *which is what his people do to gather intelligence about their guests. They then use this information to help create strong links of loyalty at his restaurants.*

> Purple Your People *is all about engaging your people. If you
> 'collect dots' about your people, you are on your way to
> creating engaged employees. Think about the things you do
> every day to collect your dots and gain Big E 'points' through
> your efforts.*

Getting the employee offer right is vital.
Understanding your team(s) helps you
to be there for them when it matters;
to create random small acts of kindness
and support, and do the things that will
create, add to or top up their 'E factor'.

We believe the key is
engaging.

The Big E and the people promise

THE
INDIVIDUAL

You no longer employ 5,
50, 500, or 5,000 'staff';
you work with
5, 50, 500, 5,000
individuals. So ban the
word 'staff' and start
talking about people.

The people promise (see Chapter 3) is a
simple term for a fab thing. It's mission,
values, leadership, culture, the collective
benefits and conditions, progression and
other variables offered by an employer
in return for a job well done. If the people promise is to drive The Big E, it
must be compelling, relevant and exciting for the employee. Most of all, it
must be clearly communicated and delivered consistently – an employer
must honour his or her promise to the workforce. The promise forms the
base of the employer brand – the 'what's in it for me' and the 'how we do
things around here' for the employee.

When we were setting up learnpurple back in 2000/2001, we asked 2,500 managers and executives in service industries what factors would most affect their likeliness to stay and progress with an employer. The results were as follows, so bear this in mind when thinking about your people offer:

1. **Communication:** two-way, adult-to-adult, consultation as well as information.

2. **Leadership:** at all levels, consistent and inspiring, support and respect.

3. **Career path:** flexible, transparent, understood and achievable.

4. **Development:** fun, useful, stimulating with a variety of delivery methods to suit the individual.

5. **Values/aspirations:** understood, respected, met with synergy between employer and employee.

There are loads of more recent studies (hit Google and you'll find them) – they'll confirm that our original research still rings true.

If you only do three things:

1
Measure engagement levels (even though this could potentially be quite scary)

2
Make clocking up engagement points a fixation

3
Deliver on your people promise

7

Clocking up Big E points before people join you

We are big fans of starting 'The Big E' way before people actually commence work with you. When someone hears about your organisation for the first time, if you've created a great place to work, people will hear about that and you'll clock up one of those Big E points mentioned in Chapter 6.

Someone sees a compelling and exciting job advert online and it encourages them to apply – (Kerching!) another engagement point.

A really friendly, helpful voice on the phone invites them in to be interviewed. (Kerching!)

The interview inspires them and they really want to join you. (Double Kerching!)

They come to a second interview and you give them feedback from their psychometric test (which they find really interesting and useful – even if they don't get the job). Also you reimburse their travelling expenses. (Enough of the Kerchings! – by now 'The Big E' is up to at least seven points).

They receive an exciting job offer from the friendly, enthusiastic voice (more points).

And then – **the wow factor** – two days later, they receive a well-thought-out induction plan full of rich experiences with set times to really get under the skin of their new organisation. This also includes:

- Some easy-to-digest notes about the organisation, its values and 'how things are done around here' handbook

- The legal stuff (e.g. their contract) so that they can think about it, and then they have it from day one

- The last newsletter or other business updates (big tick if some of this is personal to them and will help them do their job)

Clocking up Big E points before people join you

- Diary dates – social and business

- A challenge or project so that they can start achieving and feel part of the team straight away. (This could be simple stuff like researching clients or an actual project – you'd have to ask if they're OK with this first, though, as it might not always be appropriate.)

Every Friday at the Purple Palace, we all email round our top five achievements for that week so that new people – who by the way get a learnpurple email address as soon as they say 'yes' to joining us – are included straight away. They can start getting to know their colleagues and feel part of it all.

Also suggest that members of their team drop them a welcome email. It's a nice touch and more points for you.

Then if you invite your new recruit to next week's barbecue, cinema trip or whatever your fun budget allows (more about that in Chapter 16) – they're likely to attend, and you'll be well on the way to engaging your new recruit.

Doing all of that should earn you a good few Big E points!

We started doing this stuff because we're nice people and wanted to make anyone joining us feel welcome and special (because they are), but there is clearly also a big business benefit to doing it.

Imagine: if you didn't do any of this, what a huge opportunity you'd be missing . . .

Here's an example of engaging people early on

You can always tell if a company 'gets' the value of engaging people from day one. Go to the careers part of their website. If there isn't one, or if it's just a dry list of vacancies, that speaks volumes. The 'Join the team' (much better than 'Careers') page provides a golden opportunity to earn valuable Big E points. Cocktail bar chain **Be At One** *really understands the importance of The Big E. Here's some text from its website:*

'If you want to be a Professional Bartender & ooze personality you have come to the right place!

'The key to Be At One's success has been the quality of the staff and with new sites opening in London; Be At One is always on the lookout for new members to join the team.

'We only offer full-time positions (we are unable to take students) and we only consider those applications of people who have visited Be At One.

TRAINING
'When you join our team, you are assigned your very own In-Store Trainer who will train you one-on-one to be one of the best bartenders in the world. Whether you have been in the industry for five days or five years, everyone who joins the company is trained in the same way – starting at the grassroots of bartending.

'This level of training means that enthusiasm and the right attitude are more important than previous experience and we can ensure that we have a consistently excellent level of bartending across all of our sites. This process takes roughly eight weeks, but if you feel like you can turn it up a notch, you can always become a great bartender that much quicker!

STAFF DEVELOPMENT

'Our commitment to staff development through team meetings, quarterly reviews and one-on-one feedback creates opportunities and encourages upward mobility at all levels. Most members of the team stay for at least two years. In the past decade 10 of our employees have gone on to open their own bars.

'As much as we would love to place every applicant in their favourite store, we only have vacancies in some of our stores. Please choose from the list the store that you would ideally like to work in.

'We are currently fully-staffed at the moment. You can stay up-to-date by enquiring in-store and through Facebook.

WHAT'S IT REALLY LIKE WORKING FOR Be At One?

'Hi girls and guys! My name is Quentin and I'm from France. I have worked as a bartender in Be At One Hammersmith for almost a year now!

'When I look back, it's amazing for me to realise how my life has changed! I finished my studies when I was 19 and thought it could be good for me to go to London. After spending a year working in a lounge bar/club I decided to improve my level of bartending which was ridiculous. From the first day, all the B@1 team welcomed me though my English wasn't fantastic and I didn't have many bartending skills. The first three months were very hard for me and I wouldn't have stayed if the atmosphere wasn't so great! Because B@1 is all about this, every day customers have a good time because of the bartenders! What nice feedback to be surrounded with!

'As a bartender, you make the party and meet lots of people who become real friends! From the owner to your colleagues, you always push yourself to learn more and more: practising flair, learning new cocktails, attending spirit testing, training new people and, like I'm learning now, management!

'I would never have thought I could be what I am now and how brilliant it is to be a B@1 bartender! If you are looking for a job, come for a drink, see how you feel and just give it a go!'

Makes you want to work there, doesn't it?

If you only do three things:

1 Send through a well thought out induction plan and include some fun stuff

2 Send information before people join so they can hit the ground running

3 Provide a pre-work challenge to get people involved immediately and signal your achievement culture

8

Welcome in a big way:
making the most
of induction

The induction period (sometimes known in corporate speak as orientation or onboarding), is the time when a new team member is helped to settle into their new organisation and their role. Induction plays a very important part in engaging and retaining the employee so getting this right is vital.

It is in their first three critical months, that a new employee will decide one of the following:

● 'This is a place I'd like to make a real career'

● 'It's OK but not amazing, maybe I'll give it a year or so'

● 'What have I done?! This isn't at all the way they sold it – get me out of here!' (the worst case scenario)

Which of these depends on you and how your induction period is constructed.

The induction period presents a massive opportunity to 'start as you mean to go on' as well as helping set up the new joiner to succeed. It's also the time when new employees take in everything around them and are a fresh set of eyes in your organisation. Here they can offer you a bit of 'free consultancy' through their feedback and offering ideas they have to help improve your organisation.

But, more often than not, the whole process is inadequately planned, hastily executed and the opportunity is lost.

As an aspiring best place to work, you will have of course already started engagement prior to the new joiner's start date. The induction is a great opportunity to continue gaining 'engagement points' and instil a sense of belonging, loyalty and understanding in the individual, as well as setting the foundations for a successful career and optimal performance.

But how long should the induction be? How long is a piece of string? The induction should be built in the best possible way for your business, your new joiner, and the individual role; this could be one day, a week or even a month.

Here are a few examples from great companies:

Innocent

'Induction: Five days. You will learn all about the values and principles that underpin everything we do; how we make our smoothies, and the way things work around Fruit Towers (from IT stuff to working the gas BBQ in the garden).'

Links of London

'We all know how it feels to be a new starter in a new company – that's why Links of London is committed to helping you find your feet in the first few weeks. Our aim is to make sure that you feel comfortable here from day one – and that you get all the coaching you need to do your new job to the best of your abilities.

'The induction experience will vary depending on the area of the business that you join, and can range from on-the-job support from a department colleague to your line manager. It could also take the form of an individual or group induction.

'This entire process is supported by a focused HR department committed to ensuring that your career with us is as enjoyable and rewarding as possible. The HR team is available to you from day one to give guidance, offer advice and answer your questions.'

Cavendish Hotel

'At the Cavendish we understand that one size may not fit all and we are individuals with different training and development needs. Everyone when they join will be enrolled on our Hotel

Induction and will go through a departmental induction within the first four weeks. To ensure you have a full understanding of what we are about, you will also go through our two Shine programmes which will give you a full understanding of our Vision & Values, the customer journey and our approach to Service Excellence.

'We will also ensure you are provided with the skills to carry out your job, whether this is through shadowing a colleague, cross training in another department, attending a course in-house or externally.'

Inductions should be well planned in advance, written into a proper schedule and communicated to anyone who needs to know. They should also form part of the pre-joining stuff we looked at in Chapter 7. It's important to remember when planning that people can't take in vast amounts of information, so take it easy, break down the sessions and provide lots of support.

People often assume that the induction period is the responsibility of one person, namely someone in HR. However, as the information gained in this learning should cover all departments, make sure that everyone takes some responsibility and does their bit (if you have a good plan this will be clear). The line manager should hold ultimate responsibility.

In the award-winning Co-operative Financial Services call centre in Manchester, they tie helium balloons onto the back of every new starter's chair so people can come and say 'hello and welcome'. While this could potentially freak out shy types a bit, it works for them, and definitely creates a big opportunity to make people feel very welcome and welcomed.

What to include in the induction

This list is by no means exhaustive, but it should give you an idea of what to cover:

1. **Where stuff is:** layout of the building; toilets/bathrooms and other facilities; where to find a drink, lunch; their work station or locker.

2. **Culture** (see Chapter 2): 'how we do things around here', values, non-negotiables. The objective here is to gain a firm commitment that the new person is 100% happy to work within this framework (this should be OK because you will have explored it during the recruitment and selection. However, if there are any issues it's vital to uncover and resolve them now.)

3. **Meeting people:** the team, influential figures, others in the organisation, key clients, partners and others externally – the new starter should understand where they 'fit' and who to go to for help. Ideally they should have a buddy or mentor assigned at this stage who can support and smooth the settling-in period.

> Win some engagement points by providing a welcome pack. At the Purple Palace people arrive to find a collection of purple items (stationery and the like) plus a welcome card signed by all their new colleagues.

4. **Legal stuff:** this is generally a boring but necessary task, so do some fun stuff before heading here. This could include agreeing and signing the contract (which they will have had time to check when you sent it as part of the pre-joining pack), health and safety information (do it online – it's easier, quicker and on record), taking copies of work permits (you should have checked eligibility as part of the selection process), and so on.

5. **Company strategy and goals:** leading on to personal objectives so that the new starter knows exactly how to make a contribution and progress. This should apply to even the most junior job. People need to know they are part of the bigger picture and playing an important part.

6. **A bit about company history and key facts:** don't bore them to death though! Just because you find every nuance of your organisation and its long history fascinating, it doesn't mean they will. An overview will do, and then let people know where to go if they'd like to know more.

7. **Job description:** while this should have been very clear at recruitment stage, this should be discussed again so the person knows exactly what's expected. It's important at this stage to outline responsibilities, exactly what's required, what success looks like and how this can be measured.

> We always ask people how they like to be managed – this opens up positive and interesting discussion and reinforces that we treat people as individuals.

8. **Development:** on-the-job and any specialist learning so that the new starter feels he or she has the knowledge and skills to be able to deliver. Be flexible about inputs and measure outputs.

9. **Visits:** to other departments, clients, partners and so on so the joiner can get a full picture of his or her new 'world'.

10. **Team-building activities:** both work and social.

11. **Project:** this is a great time to harness a person's creativity and get to know them better as well as getting something useful done.

12. **Psychometric feedback:** in our view using psychometrics as part of the selection process and/or at this stage is a no-brainer.

> You know the first few months when new people are finding their feet and you're figuring out how to get the best out of them? Well, psychometrics really can save time and minimise conflict at this vital stage. And if you do this for the whole team/department, everyone knows how best to work together and support each other.

There's a lot here, so you can see how doing induction properly could be time consuming. But the advantages far outweigh the effort – for any organisation – so prioritise your schedule and plan carefully. Be aware of giving too much too soon and communicate at an appropriate level to the individual; keep it real. There's an example of a purple induction plan at www. purpleyourpeople.com (see Chapter 23 for details on how to access this).

Once you have your induction in place and the new team member is taking everything on board, it's so very important to make sure there are regular one-to-one meetings diarised to:

● Review progress

● Answer questions

● Provide development

● Harness ideas and feedback

● And for loads of other good reasons

However, this is something that often falls off the bottom of the busy line manager's to-do list. Don't let it. How often is up to you: just make sure it happens! A tried and tested way is to review as follows:

● At the end of weeks one, two, three and four

● Then at the end of months two and three

● Then decide what's appropriate – it's all about the individual, remember

Some people will require more input than others, or you may have more to do with them; it's just a case of judging the situation. Of course you'll be meeting to discuss the day-to-day stuff anyway, so it may well be that you build your reviews into that. If you do, though, make sure you record actions and are clear that you are carrying out a thorough and properly structured review, such as the one we have included below. You don't have to adhere to this structure; keep it flexible as only you know where the conversation will take you. Just be sure to cover all points and ask open questions so you end up listening more than you talk. The idea is to coach the person to their own conclusions rather than doing lots of 'telling':

1. How's it going for you? (Listen, probe, think.)

2. On a scale of one to 10, with one being miserable and 10 being ecstatic, how do you feel right now?

3. What would make you an 8, 9, 10?

4. Anything you need to help you do your job better? (This might be resources, time, development – if you can't make them available, face the issues and discuss how you can both make things work better.)

4. Any feedback about the organisation, ideas, suggestions?

5. Once you've thoroughly explored these points, give your feedback on their achievements/progress to date and initiate a two-way discussion on what's been achieved.

6. Explore and agree actions and discuss the 'hows' if the person would welcome your support or input (remember, they might not).

7. Record the review (or, better still, ask them to do so and send you a copy).

Two ways to make tough feedback more appetising

1. Use a pre-emptive statement such as 'You might not want to hear this, though . . .' or 'I know you want to be the best at what you do, so . . .' or 'I wouldn't be doing my job properly if I didn't tell you . . .'

2. The good old-fashioned feedback sandwich:

Good feedback> things you could do better>good feedback

'I really liked the tone of the report, though there needs to be much more evidence to back up your points. Overall though, I know it's going to be great.'

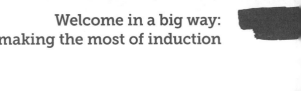

If you only do three things:

1
Start as you mean to go on. Set the scene and clarify expectations on both sides

2
Involve all relevant people in the induction process and make the welcome a big one

3
Build in reviews throughout and make sure they happen

9

The Big C:
communication

The Big C: communication

Most employee survey results show 'communication' as a key area for improvement because few organisations get it right. And even after the survey has highlighted an issue, few businesses strive to solve it in the best way possible.

So it's not an accident that this is the longest chapter in this book because 'The Big C' is a massive area, which has a huge impact.

When we conducted our initial research for setting up learnpurple, communication showed up as the top motivator for people in service industries. People said they wanted to be involved and consulted, not just on the receiving end of 'telling'. They said they wanted to be able to influence what's going on around them and have a say in the big decisions. **Overall, they just wanted two-way ongoing communication.** Doesn't sound all that hard, does it?

But if you ask any employee how they'd rate internal communication on a scale of one to 10 (with 10 being brilliant), you'd be lucky to raise a five. So is it more difficult than originally thought? Is that why so few organisations get it right?

Top five motivators at work

1. Communication

2. Leadership

3. Career path

4. Development/ progression

5. Values/culture

Source: learnpurple original research

The answer is no: communication just takes time and effort – hence why many organisations are put off investing in it. Getting it right, however, can have a considerable influence on the motivation, performance and productivity of people and is a huge contributor to The Big E (employee engagement) so perhaps one to keep on your priority list!

We could have written a whole book on The Big C (and may actually do so), but we wanted to make this section as simple to follow as possible, so here's our rough guide.

The Big E

The Big C

The big picture approach

Employees expect to be treated with respect, want to enjoy an adult-to-adult relationship with their manager and employer, to have a voice and to be able to influence their own progress and environment. They also need to have the information to enable them to deliver an excellent job, keep in the know, remain inspired and to know how they are doing. This is all fair enough, but with everything moving so much faster than even five years ago and the challenges of daily business life increasing, for many it seems impossible to keep everyone up to speed with what's going on and happy in their work.

Our big picture take on this is for managers and leaders to stop making the decisions that influence people's lives and start valuing and trusting their people enough to keep them in the picture. To treat people with respect and hand over the responsibility to those who are 'doing the doing'. So instead of sitting in the boardroom deciding stuff, then doing some telling and expecting information to cascade downwards (through that often murky middle-management layer), we believe it's better for leaders to consult and involve people from the bottom up. This way they will know what's going on and will buy in to the decisions made. And let me tell you a little secret – **the people who are doing the doing often have the best ideas** – ideas that can boost sales and profit or save you lots of money. So why would you not access this valuable 'free' resource?

Of course you're going to come up against the 'knowledge = power' brigade who believe they're the best people (in some cases the only people) to bring about change and make decisions.

An example of consultation

Kwik-Fit Financial Services has an award-winning rewards and benefits strategy which evolved largely by consulting and involving its people. As a call centre organisation with a high number of young, low-paid employees, this insurance intermediary looked to its benefits strategy to help overcome a number of wider business issues. A key part of this was to hold many consultation groups. Some of the resulting benefits included unusual and extensive on-site facilities such as a full-time staff concierge service, a fully equipped gym with a full-time personal trainer, and more flexibility over holiday time taken. In 2009, the company also invested a six-figure sum in creating a chill-out zone for its people, with plasma TVs and games consoles, a coffee and smoothie bar, internet access and two US-style pool tables.

The organisation's flexible benefits scheme includes a wide range of perks, such as dental insurance, private medical insurance, retail vouchers, holiday trading and bikes for work. To help with annual benefits selections, the company holds workshops, run by independent tax advisers, which people are given time to attend during the working day. These are provided free of charge – fairly unusual in most industry sectors.

Since the strategy was introduced, absence levels reduced year-on-year from 6.8% in 2005 to 3.5% in 2009, and labour turnover fell from 40% in 2004 to 22% in 2009. Recruitment costs also dropped, with more direct applications as a result of word of mouth.

And as fewer people aspire to hold management and leadership positions, it's going to become increasingly important to enable the workforce to self-manage and have decision making skills and authority. At learnpurple we call this 'freedom within a framework'.

This is how it can work:

1. Make sure the big picture goals and strategy are clear to all

2. Decide the non-negotiables

3. Make sure your values are firmly embedded and part of daily life – they are your 'police force' (see Chapter 2)

4. Leaders must 'walk the talk'

5. Ensure people are clear on roles, responsibilities, targets and metrics

6. Measure outputs instead of inputs

7. Define resources and budgets

8. Decide how the consultation process will work and what sort of things require formal sign-off

9. Make sure support is always available and people know how to access it

10. Be prepared to accept change, different approaches and new ways of thinking

There's always going to be a need for good communication, so here's a short road map.

Very important fact

The people who are at the sharp end usually know best. You don't employ children, you employ grown-ups who have mortgages, relationships, children and out-of-work responsibilities, activities and talents like you wouldn't believe. So trust, respect, consult, listen, learn and be amazed.

Planning

Who: whether spoken, written or otherwise, communication must be crafted with the recipient in mind. Use language they'll 'get' and think about how best to 'sell' what you're saying, asking or consulting on. Use real examples and stories to make it real. Think also about who's the best person to do the communicating.

> Thinking things through into 'virtual bullet points' can help.

How: what's the best method and how will you execute it?

Style: formal or otherwise, clarity is key – what is it you actually want to consult on and/or convey?

Outcomes: the ideal result(s) from the communication. How will everyone know they're 'there'?

Method: the best way to give and receive information in any particular instance. Get your facts right.

> Sometimes it helps to write down and/or play out the communication in your head or with a friend.

When: timing is critical – when's the best time? Allow adequate time – if you need to move fast, do it.

Actions: next steps and follow-up required.

Face-to-face/Skype/phone conversations

- If possible, give advance notice so that people know what to expect

- Remember respect, trust and the adult-to-adult relationship

- Be clear

- Listen: consult first and listen instead of telling (ask open questions – see Chapter 5)

- Check understanding and make sure expectations are clear; take notes

- Agree the way forward and how required outcomes will be evidenced

- You might want to follow up by email or text

- End on a positive, upbeat note

- Do what you said you'd do as a result (under-promise, over-deliver) – that means putting the actions into your diary or on to today's or tomorrow's to-do list right away

A word about meetings

Some people have meetings for meetings' sake. Or unproductive meetings that go on too long, bore everyone to death and achieve very little. Sometimes there are people who love the sound of their own voice or just like having a rant chairing the session.

Hint: if you don't feel excited about going to a meeting, the other parties won't either – do something about this.

Conducted well, meetings can be dynamite (in a good way).

Decide what needs to be covered and the outcomes you want to see – then plan a timed agenda (or better still, let go and ask one of the attendees to chair and plan – then you don't have to and they'll feel more trusted, in the know and are highly likely to do a great job).

Record action points only – what, who, when, what if (and possibly, though not necessarily), how.

Presenting to a group

Who: think about the group and what will get them excited and interested – talk their language, think of stories and examples they'll relate to. Each person takes in information differently, whether verbally, visually or through feeling or doing. Try to ensure there is something for everyone.

> Read the mood in the room – are people listening, nodding their heads (or otherwise)? Adapt your approach to keep them interested and on your side. You can't do this if you're reading from lots of notes, so learn how to speak from the heart, using notes as a prompt.

What: be clear and make sure you can fit all key points into the time available.

How: if you must use slides, use images to illustrate your point and, if appropriate and at all possible, bring in some humour. Never read out text from a slide (and I mean **never**, unless you're referring to figures, tables, etc.). Keep it simple, high-impact and energetic.

Interact with the audience: talk to them as if you're having a conversation – expect and encourage them to answer back. Check they're still 'with you', check understanding, and seek feedback – 'Does that make sense?' 'How does that look/sound/feel to you?'

And remember, practice makes perfect. If you know your stuff and can communicate it clearly, it is more likely the audience will be engaged, will interact and will take action following the meeting.

Email

1.   Before you write an email, consider whether a phone call or face-to-face meeting would give you a better and/or quicker result (and provide an opportunity for a bit of bonding).

2.   Email is for quick replies, so reply quickly (our rule at the Purple Palace is by the end of the day). If something requires more attention and can't be dealt with that day, reply to say when you'll be dealing with it, diarise it and do it.

3.   Be disciplined to deal with email every day. Make sure that by the end of the day you have no more emails in your inbox than are

visible without scrolling down. Be organised and don't become a slave to email to the detriment of progressing other work, though – there is an off button.

4. Use the subject bar properly to make it very clear what the email is about, e.g. instead of 'Budget' write 'January 2012 budget (info)'. Only use 'Urgent' or a red flag if it really is – in which case phone or face-to-face is probably better.

5. This will save loads of time. Consider putting your message into the subject bar only so that the recipient doesn't even have to open the email. In this case you need seven small but powerful words to use in brackets after the message:

● Saw a great accountant and appointed today **(End)**

● Bar and restaurant budget figures need re-forecasting due to second Michelin star **(Action)**

● Sales figures 40% up **(Info)**

● Attending the budget meeting? **(Confirm)**

● We screwed up the budget figures we're presenting tomorrow – when can you meet? **(Urgent)**

● Group budget **(Summary)**

● Pub on Thursday after budget meeting **(Social)**

6. Keep text short and focused, use bullet points and always make it clear what you require as a response. Read through before you send for a sense check. Emails to clients and head office should be checked carefully.

7. Use email for positive messages only; problems should be dealt with by other means. Keep the tone even and friendly yet professional. NEVER USE CAPITALS – THEY SHOUT!

8. Never write anything you wouldn't want to see on the front page of the local paper or that you wouldn't say to someone's face. If there's something sensitive to deal with, don't do it by email.

9. Think before you 'cc' (copy people in) – only send messages to those who really need to know to avoid clogging up people's inboxes. Ditto with the 'reply to all' function.

10. Only attach items that are essential. If people are on BlackBerry, post short attachments into the email under the main message.

Bonus tip: delete all spam, chain letters, jokes and unknown attachments – never forward them on.

Social media

I'm not going to go into detail here: suffice it to say anything broadcast via a social networking site like Twitter, LinkedIn, Facebook and YouTube can potentially be seen by the whole world, so take care and use them to your advantage.

You could set up a group for your employees, which could significantly enhance the communication process. You have to maintain it, though, and make sure it's fed with rich content, otherwise it's better to leave well alone.

If you only do three things:

1 Encourage and expect everyone to be responsible for communicating

2 Create 'freedom within a framework' and get people deciding for themselves

3 Think before you communicate

10

Employee opinion:
the power of the people

If you're not just dipping into this book and have read the previous chapters, you'll know by now that finding out what people think and feel is the first step towards being a great place to work and employing inspired, happy and more profitable people. If, as an organisation, you're diligently clocking up those employee engagement points, you and your fellow leaders, managers and supervisors will be interacting regularly with your people and finding out what they think. There are times, though, when you might want to take a 'snapshot' of what everyone thinks about a range of issues – or perhaps one specific topic – and that's when employee surveys can come in handy.

You should only ever run a survey if:

1. You feel you're culturally ready to deal with this type of intervention.

2. You're prepared to take the feedback on the chin (bearing in mind some of it might not be all that positive), without recriminations.

3. You're going to act on it (or some of it) and if some things can't change, you're willing to honestly explain why.

4. You're prepared to communicate what you've learned and what you're going to do about it in a very transparent way.

> Employee surveys do not replace dialogue – they should promote and support it.
>
> In smaller organisations, just ask people.

Response rates

We reckon a good, well-publicised online survey should yield about a 30–40% completion rate.

If you do a great job on the first one, though, showing everyone what actions you've taken as a result and how this has made business improvements, it can help make the response rate shoot up next time. The Pizza Express employee opinion survey 'The People Express', which we ran in 2011, had over 70% responses – and this was because they'd done a top job at acting on the previous set of results.

Employee opinion: the power of the people

Employee surveys not only find out what people think, they let people know that you care what they think – which is very important. Again this only works if you act on the results.

In line with our 'keep it simple' value, avoid long boring surveys that are hard to fill in. This 'spray and pray' approach is confusing for everyone and gives too much detailed data, which you're unlikely to have the time or resources to really analyse and deal with.

Make your survey visually attractive and on brand. Use pictures. Keep the language simple and contemporary. For best results consult a professional – there's a science and art behind constructing smart questions.

For a simple example, take a look at our q-box survey at www. purpleyourpeople.com (free for 100 people or fewer).

Our own learnpurple survey is on brand:

Chapter 10

The why

Of course you'll be working towards a situation where people want to have their say and will openly contribute because they know you'll take their feedback on board and do something with it. If you've not yet reached that particular nirvana, you may need to offer an incentive. Some organisations offer vouchers or give a donation to charity for every survey completed. **We like surveys that are fun to do and offer a reward at the end.** For example, the first online Pizza Express survey we produced had a piece of video footage at the end (only visible once all the questions had been answered) where the CEO and Operations Director were 'playing their air guitars' and people got to vote for who did it best. Cheap to do, fun and oddly compelling.

Content

Instead of finding someone else's survey on the web and copying that, you could work with an expert who will help you design something perfect for your organisation. Alternatively, sit down and think hard about what it is you want to improve and therefore what information you actually need to find out. The sort of topics you might look to cover could include:

1. How happy and/or satisfied and/or engaged people are

2. Culture/values: whether people know them, live them, align with them

3. Brand

4. Roles and responsibilities

5. Leadership management

6. Strategy/goal alignment

7. Environment

8. CSR

9. Reward and recognition

Employee opinion: the power of the people

10. Ability to fulfil contribution

11. Your performance as an employer

12. Communication

13. Change

14. Ideas and innovations

15. Information about the person responding

> We love happy scales – you can compare departments, sites, regions etc; you can benchmark over time. Happy is not a fluffy measure – if you really think about it; it's a tough indicator of the state of your organisation.

It's a bit more interesting if you vary the type of question:

Scales

Do you feel listened to at work? 1 ☐ 2 ☐ 3 ☐ 4 ☐ 5 ☐ 6 ☐ 7 ☐ 8 ☐ 9 ☐ 10

1 = Never, I feel like I am ignored

10 = Yes, my manager always listens to me and values my opinion

Yes/no (closed questions)

Would you recommend Company XYZ to others as a great place to work? ☐ Yes ☐ No

Radio buttons

Please tell us how you think we are living our priorities

	Ouch!	Needs watching	On track	Wow!
Demonstrating a passion for life	☐	☐	☐	☐
Engaging the customer	☐	☐	☐	☐
Showing a generous spirit	☐	☐	☐	☐
Caring about people	☐	☐	☐	☐
Implementing brilliantly	☐	☐	☐	☐

Drop-down menus or lists

Finally, the most important bit, what do you do? | Senior Manager ∨

Director
Senior Manager
Middle Manager
Junior Manager
Sales Executive
Sales Administrator

Text boxes: keep free text to a minimum, as it's difficult to analyse

What do you care about in work and/or life?

If you're going to the time and expense of running an employee survey, you need to make sure that the leadership team are on board and behind the initiative. Showing that it is supported from the very top will encourage others to get involved.

To be anonymous or not to be: that is the confidentiality question

If you're promoting trust and openness and people feel confident to say what they think, then it makes sense to support this by not going down the anonymous route. However, if you're not there yet and really want people to express themselves fully without fear of recriminations, then choose the anonymous option and make sure

Unless you really have very restricted access to technology (and remember there are internet cafes and free wireless all over the place), conducting your survey online is a no-brainer. It's easy to access, quicker to do and the big bonus is that results are instantaneous. The world moves too fast to be waiting weeks for survey results. You want to put your energy into resolving the issues that surface, not manually collecting and collating data, which, by the time it's ready, is probably already out of date.

the survey really is totally confidential and preferably analysed by a third party.

The outcomes

Avoid reports that are thicker than the London *Yellow Pages* and make you feel as though you're drowning in data – you won't have time to do them justice. Ideally use a company that will collate and summarise the information and make recommendations for you. Our outline action plan for handling the outcomes would be:

1. Draw up a clear communications plan for sharing the results.

   (a) Top line: overall 'what's good and what could we do better', plus a few quirky facts to add interest and a clear indicator of the action plan going forward;

   (b) By team: ensure each manager is fully briefed on giving their department specific feedback and facilitating action-planning discussions so that the team can own the data and follow up action.

2. Acknowledge points that can't be changed and explain the rationale.

3. Work on no more than three big actions as an organisation and communicate throughout.

4. Find some quick wins – smaller, easy to do, low-cost/no-cost things that will win you some engagement points. Deliver them and let everyone know.

5. Deliver the agreed larger actions ahead of time and shout about that too.

If you only do three things:

1
Involve leaders and make sure everyone's prepared to deal with the feedback like adults

2
If you use a survey, make it fun and engaging

3
Take action so that people know it's worth giving the feedback next time

11

The Halfway Man

You're now about halfway through this book, so time for a true story about the **'Halfway Man'**.

There once was a CEO who loved business books. His office walls were lined with shelves spilling over with them. He read every title he could get his hands on.

BUT he only ever read the first half. So everyone called him the 'Halfway Man'.

By the halfway point of each book, he figured he'd got the message and knew enough to be able to use the ideas within. As a result, he was forever introducing new initiatives and ways of working.

His people were in turmoil. They liked the Halfway Man and knew he was trying to make things better.

But in his enthusiasm to implement the stuff he'd learned from his half books, he was creating chaos. His people were very frustrated and lacked any sort of clarity or direction.

He was inconsistent in his approach, because, of course, many of the books contained contradictory points of view.

And because he never reached the end of any one book he didn't have the full information.

In his haste to digest so many books he never stopped to really think about the contents.

When the executive team challenged the Halfway Man, he quoted bits of his books at them, believing that because something appeared in a book, it would be the right thing to do for him and his organisation.

Things were always changing in the Halfway Man's organisation. His poor, long-suffering teams made the most of things, weathering numerous storms and, even though they loved the work, many ended up leaving or on long-term sick leave.

The Halfway Man

Eventually the Halfway Man had to pack up his books and move on. This was a positive thing for the organisation, and he did find a new role – let's just hope he learned from his halfway experience.

> So don't be the halfway man (or woman): finish this book and think carefully about how the things you've learned could work within your specific organisation.

There's a chapter later on to help you do this.

12

Managing performance

So you've put all this effort into attracting, selecting, engaging and canvassing opinion from talented people who will enhance your organisation, all of which are very important assets. But you also need to think about their performance in the company. This chapter is about balancing, nurturing and developing the individual while fulfilling the needs of team and organisation. It's a balance that is equitable.

Suppose you're a chef and you'd laid out a small fortune on white Alba truffles, then you just threw them on a shelf in a plastic bag and didn't think twice about them. Or you spent a fortune on vintage McQueen and then left it in a heap in a damp corner of your warehouse, gathering dust for months . . . In reality you'd be lovingly encasing your truffle in fresh paper and sealing it in a jar in the fridge, or cleaning, wrapping and carefully storing your couture clothes; in the same way it's your job to nurture your people assets as you would any other business asset; helping them to be the best they can be. Think hard about that for a minute.

People who are happy, progressing on a daily basis and working towards their potential will be more inspired, motivated, engaged and productive; therefore more profitable and will stay with you longer. With remarkably few exceptions, there are no bad employees, just mismatched ones, poor management and/or a defective organisation.

Assuming you've made goals and expectations very clear from the outset so that all team members know what they're there to do (see Chapter 2), it's easy to manage performance. They're either producing the required outcomes, or they're not. There should be no surprises.

A number of important things to think about when managing performance:

1. **Trust and belief:** if you're recruiting properly and taking on people you're truly excited about, you owe it to them to:

    Purple people truly believe that you reap what you sow when it comes to managing people.

    (a) Believe they can fulfil the role
    (b) Trust them to get on with it.

Chapter 12

This is where the adult-to-adult relationship factor comes in. Given that you don't employ children (unless you're reading this in a country where that's allowed, in which case please stop right now and find a better way), there's no reason people should let you down.

2. **Support:** provide the framework, tools, resources and development and be on hand if people need help or guidance. Then stand back and light the blue touch paper . . .

3. **Respect:** people might do something differently from the way you do (or did) it and that's OK – as long as they fulfil your values and are doing things legally and ethically. Remember it's all about the results.

4. **Feedback:** people need to know how they're doing (praise as well as correction). This is key – make sure people have ongoing feedback, especially during the settling-in period. Sometimes managers 'let little stuff go' and then they get to a stage where things are out of control and conflict happens. To deal with uncomfortable situations, use the feedback options in Chapter 8. If you've been smart and allocated a buddy or mentor, they'll be providing feedback and support in a more natural, less official way, which is a good thing.

Speak to the one

Sometimes when there is an issue, people gripe about it to one another. This is very bad news. Make it a rule, an unshakeable part of your framework, that if there are issues, people speak only to the person who can bring about the necessary change. It's a great imperative for life – try it, we know you'll like it. (This also works if you want to get rid of a gossip culture.)

5. **Team excellence:** train people to 'police' the standard of the work they produce so that they are self-regulating and self-supporting. An inspired and proud team doing a great job simply won't allow someone to let the side down.

6. **Openness:** encourage people to ask questions, raise minor issues and ask for help. Make it part of your culture.

7. **Consistency:** it's really important to treat people fairly and offer them the same level of support and tolerance to all.

Handling difficult feedback

There is no difficult feedback if you've taken care to clearly lay out all the ground rules. However, if you're in a situation where you're worried about having a challenging discussion or potential conflict, use the review technique described in Chapter 8.

You'll need to be clear about:

- Where we are now (with good examples to evidence the shortfalls)

- Where we want to get to (what a good job looks like, how we'll know)

- What factors are causing the gaps (you'll need to probe)

- How we're going to get there (ask, support, discuss)

- What support or resource might be needed

- Agreed actions – firm commitment from all parties

Take a deep breath, be honest and matter of fact. This is definitely not a time to be emotional, but don't leave your empathy at home that day either.

A true story: the operations manager was amazed

Harry had gone to the operations director's office to complain about Grace, an underperforming team member who just wasn't pulling her weight and kept dissolving into tears.

OD: 'So, Harry, what are you going to do about it?'

Harry: 'Well. I thought I'd wait till her end of month review and then performance manage her.'

OD: 'How about we talk with her right now? She's obviously unhappy – let's find out why.'

Grace came in and clammed up to start with. The OD explained that she just wanted to help, knowing that it's impossible to perform well when so clearly unhappy. Instead of admonishing the non-conformances and drilling down into the detail, what happened next was a very empathetic, adult-to-adult conversation, after which Grace said:

'I think I've made a massive mistake, I love the company and all you stand for; it's just the work that's wrong for me. I've thought about whether there's another role here for me but there just isn't. And I feel bad because I don't want to let people down. I'm so relieved we're talking like this.'

As a result, they helped Grace to find her perfect job elsewhere. Everyone was happy with the outcome and the unpleasant, disruptive nature of formal performance management was completely avoided.

Harry was amazed and delighted that the OD had taken such a proactive stance and resolved an issue he'd been worrying about for weeks.

Of course you'd have to take care that the informal chat doesn't turn into a potential disciplinary situation or could be construed as constructive dismissal, in which case stop immediately and follow your organisation's formal procedure. There are times though when a straightforward empathetic and exploratory conversation can help avoid a whole lot of hassle.

If you only do three things:

1 Nurture and support to enable your people to be the best they can be

2 Believe and trust, cultivating adult-to-adult relationships

3 Be very clear from the outset about what's required and 'how we do things around here'

13

Talent review

T he talent review in a simple form is all about succession planning, creating a leadership pipeline and making sure you have the right people in the right roles at the right time.

This includes:

- Reviewing performance, aspirations and potential (bearing in mind that everyone has potential, so the skill is finding the right path for each individual)

- Assessing readiness for progression plus development needs

- Identifying the people required for the success of the organisation now and in the future, identifying gaps and working towards filling these (internally or externally)

- Making sure that there is a fair, transparent and consistent way of facilitating all of the above

Reviews and appraisals

Ask 500 people in a room to put their hand up if they've had an enjoyable and productive performance appraisal in the last year and you'll be lucky to get into double figures (we know, we do this all the time when speaking at conferences).

Reviews and appraisals are something people know they should do, sort of know how to do but then always seem to fall off the bottom of their to-do lists. Managers almost universally dislike appraisal time and try to avoid it. They find appraisals time-consuming and daunting, and feel that little value results.

Formal appraisal is not just an opportunity to manage performance, but is also the perfect time to:

- Give positive feedback

- Say thank you for a job well done

Chapter 13

- Show gratitude for discretionary effort

- Help people fulfil their contribution

- Discuss development

- Harness ideas and feedback

- Plan for the future

- Help clarify the way forward

- Re-motivate, re-invigorate and inspire

> One-to-ones are a real opportunity to develop a productive, professional relationship. As well as the business stuff, get to know each other as people, tell company stories, talk about the latest sitcom, family, sport . . . whatever floats your boat. You'll also clock up a few engagement points while you're at it.

Part of the challenge is that people aren't managing performance and other issues as they go along (see Chapter 12). Only by having regular one-to-ones (some call them 'coffee chats') will trust be developed between parties. If they know each other well on a business level then it stands to reason they'll be able to have richer, more enjoyable and productive one-to-ones when the time comes.

The point of an appraisal is to have a rich one-to-one discussion with productive and inspiring outcomes.

But . . .

Everything flows so fast and people are bombarded with everyday information, so if they spend time and effort conducting reviews and appraisals, business pressures tend to take over and somehow writing them up is forgotten. Or they're recorded three months later when the detail of the conversation has been forgotten (and people say 'was I actually *in* this meeting?'). Or the notes are lost. Or what's been agreed is quickly out of date.

An HR director friend, let's call him Vaughn, told me about his first day in a new role. He was out on site visits with the site general manager.

Vaughn: 'Who's that over there?'

Manager: 'Fred.'

Vaughn: 'What's his surname?'

Manager: 'Don't know.'

Vaughn: 'How long's Fred been here?'

Manager: 'Don't know.'

Vaughn: 'What's his development plan?'

Manager: 'Don't know.'

You get the picture. I'm not making this up – it happens all the time in fast-growth businesses.

The solution is to find a system whereby goals and other outcomes are properly recorded and easily accessible, then regularly updated and reviewed throughout the year. So the appraisal becomes the responsibility of the individual, not his or her manager, and it can move from an annual one-off exercise to an ongoing, flowing way of progressing. Fantastic!

There's much research to prove that progression is a top motivator – I'd go one further and say it's a basic human need. Growing the whole person not just developing them to deliver the needs of the business will reap rewards. You can't grow people if you don't understand them and aren't able to treat each one as an individual.

The easy way to making this happen: part of my story

One of the main reasons I left my challenging and well-paid MD's role in 2001 to start learnpurple was my light bulb moment.

I thought that if people could find a way of automating the administration and management of appraisals and review, so as to be able to put their efforts into actually conducting great one-to-ones and then making the outcomes happen, this would be a very good thing.

I came up with talent toolbox™, which is our web-enabled talent management system. Having seen this in action for 10 years now I have to say that automating your talent management is a complete no-brainer. In-house system, learnpurple's or someone else's; do it now – the return on investment (ROI) is huge. (See case studies at www.learnpurple.com.)

Imagine you could know, at the touch of a button:

- Exactly who's working for you and where

- What their role and responsibilities entail

- Details of their last appraisal and one-to-ones

- What their skills and knowledge are

- How well they're performing

- Whether they're on track to meet goals and objectives

- How these goals link to strategic intent

- How they could develop and improve

- What their potential is likely to be

- How likely they are to stay or leave and when

- How happy and engaged they are

- What their aspirations are

- How they're going to progress

- Where they're heading and who will replace them

- What they think about your organisation

- What ideas they have

- How they think and feel about work

ROI from online talent management systems is derived from:

- Reduced recruitment costs (better succession planning)

- More accurate development needs analysis (see Chapter 18)

- Time savings

- Improved performance management

- People driving their own progress

- More focused, goal-oriented people

- Activity aligned to strategy

- Improved engagement and retention

- Enhanced productivity

- More trust and openness

- Increased feeling of ownership

- People feel invested in and more valued

- Ideas generated

- Decreased conflict/grievances

- Market reputation – more job applications

And if you incorporate your employee opinion survey, that's a cost saved too.

Although there are best practice appraisal content formats (we have many) it's important that content is totally aligned; to fit the needs of the individual organisation, strategy and key metrics as well as its culture and its people.

Self review

It's vital that people have an opportunity to review their own progress before meeting with their line manager. Both parties should do some planning and then come together to discuss the results. You can imagine how, with an online system, this would be easy to facilitate.

Formal performance assessment

Some people use competencies like this:

Or objectives, which could be strategic or personal like this:

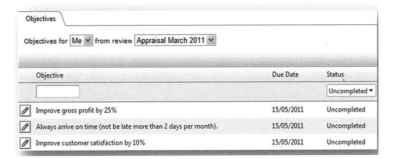

Sometimes there are universal key performance indicators (KPIs) like this:

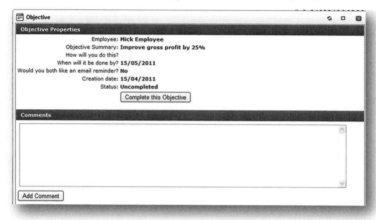

Or they measure against values or business principles.

Or a combination.

The important thing is to keep things simple, clear and unambiguous.

Remember: the point of the appraisal or review is all about having a fantastically rich, future-focused conversation, not about sweating the small stuff and box-ticking.

We'd strongly recommend that to turn the appraisal one-to-one into a positive adult-to-adult conversation, some of the softer opinion and aspirational areas should be explored. The goal here is a well-rounded and rich conversation that explores all aspects of the individual's interaction with the organisation.

For example, using a 'happy scale' of one to 10 can prompt an open and honest discussion as well as providing a great benchmark metric to use to assess the status quo and ongoing progress of team, group, division, region and company.

Another example would be to ask people 'What next?' to open up a conversation about the future in a non-threatening way.

In tough times or periods of change and uncertainty

During uncertain times many organisations put off their appraisals because they find the approach more difficult than when everything is going well. However, this is exactly when a rich and honest one-to-one is most critical.

Managers should be encouraged to continue holding appraisals. But in order to do so, they need to be given extra support. Make sure they are up to date and informed about the latest situation and coached in the skills that are required to communicate this, especially if the update is not going to be an easy tell. It may also be that they do not feel they have the time to effectively plan and carry out an appraisal. Or they may be feeling pretty down themselves and the will to listen to others is eroded. So make sure they are also given the opportunity to air their views and are really listened to.

No matter how tough the economy, or how foggy the future, people still need to have a chance to talk about their personal aspirations and progress. It's the role of business owners and leaders to ensure that managers can carry out these appraisals and are not afraid to do so. The future success of the organisation may well depend on them.

360° appraisal – proceed with caution

As well as self-assessment and feedback from the line manager, this all-round view provides feedback from colleagues, the person's own team and maybe, though far less frequently, even from external partners such as suppliers or customers.

Used with care, 360° appraisal can be a very useful tool. However, it's vital to use it responsibly and under the right conditions, i.e. within a culture that's ready to deal with it. Trust, openness and a willingness to give and accept feedback have to be in place. Confidentiality is paramount and managers have to undergo comprehensive training to be able to give feedback in the correct way.

At learnpurple we spend quite a bit of time talking people out of using the 360° process. Why? Because culturally they're not ready for it; or they don't understand the potential implications; there is prevailing distrust of management; or they aren't prepared to train their managers in coaching and feedback skills to a high enough level or to invest in skilled coaches to assist with the feedback process.

We'd recommend you only consider implementing 360° appraisals if:

- The organisation already has a well-established and trusted review process in place and so extending it to a 360° approach would be a logical and welcome next step.

- It is carried out fairly and sensitively, with full support around the outcomes.

- The individual is able to 'own' the process and therefore feel in control rather than having something 'done to them'.

Unfortunately, we've been brought in at the back end of disaster whereby well-meaning leadership teams have decided to adopt 360° without full understanding and experience, and then had to deal with the fallout. In short, how it could work well is:

- Approximately eight people, for example peers, subordinates, members of the leadership team, provide feedback describing an individual's performance.

- Often the individual and his or her line manager fill in a questionnaire too.

- Ideally the feedback process should be anonymous so that summary information is available but no one knows 'who said what'.

- The feedback is presented to the recipient by a skilled coach or well-trained manager.

We've been developing award-winning talent management systems for almost 10 years and have come up with a way to incorporate 360° feedback into the regular appraisal process. This makes for an efficient and effective review.

There's a bit of a 360° bandwagon at the moment. People read or hear about it, feel it would be good for their business and then find a 'free trial' via the internet or other quick and easy solution. Managed and implemented well, 360° feedback can significantly enhance performance. However, if it is suddenly introduced out of the blue and/or perceived to be in any way threatening, it can seriously damage engagement, performance and retention.

Once the review process is in place and working, the hard work is done. A well-crafted system will provide everything you need to carry out a first-class talent review; thus planning for future business needs, making the most of the talent you have in place and enabling the necessary development, recruitment and activity required.

If you only do three things:

1

Make regular appraisals and ongoing reviews part of your DNA, putting the work in to enable really rich one-to-one discussions

2

Make appraisals a positive event, enabling people to drive their own progress

3

Use a great system to plan for the future

14

Leaders at all levels

L eadership isn't just about the inspirational and visionary CEO. To the person on the front line, their manager is the leader, exemplifying what the company is all about. We therefore believe that to have any chance at all of getting the people stuff right, organisations must create leaders at all levels.

When organisations come to us with limited learning and development budgets, we advise them to develop their middle managers because that's where the investment is likely to show the most return (apart, perhaps, from customer service because sales always increase straight away). If, hand on heart, your leaders (at all levels) aren't up to scratch, it's time to take action.

> Leaders can ask themselves: 'If there was a leadership election tomorrow, would I win?'

Often with leadership you see a cascade effect – great leadership breeds great leadership and vice versa. Senior types and business owners need to make sure they are displaying role model behaviours and excellent leadership qualities to ensure that their managers, and the managers of the future, exert what the company needs.

However, this alone is not enough.

Characteristics of a good leader

There are many, so here's a checklist to get you thinking. You could use this to decide which traits are most important for your environment and teams. Great leaders are complex beings. You can't expect all leaders at all levels to display all of these traits.

What's important is that they're not routinely displaying the opposite behaviours because that would cause a lot of damage.

> Poor managers used to be able to hide behind their status. These days information flow is freer, expectations are higher and people aren't going to 'put up and shut up'. People expect, and have a right to, decent leadership.

Start now at improving leadership capability at all levels – develop the following, as appropriate. Decide the most important for your organisation and work on one or two at a time; you'll be on the way to improving leadership capability within your organisation.

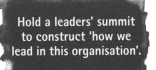

Hold a leaders' summit to construct 'how we lead in this organisation'.

Doing nothing is a decision and usually a poor choice.

✔ **Clarity:** being able to 'unravel the spaghetti', see the big picture and make sense of complex situations. Then being able to articulate clearly.

✔ **Decisiveness:** problem-solving and decision-making are important traits. It's better to make a decision and then adapt and amend than procrastinate. Decisions force action, which brings about progression.

✔ **Vision:** the ability to look forward in an enlightened and open-minded way; to be strategic yet pragmatic.

✔ **Courage:** of convictions and bravery to take the tough decisions, make calculated risks and face harsh challenges.

✔ **Action-centred:** the ability to 'make it happen', bringing things to a conclusion, leaving no loose ends.

✔ **Respect:** capable of giving it and earning it.

✔ **Flexibility and adaptability:** because there are few constants in life and the ability to champion change is key.

✔ **Consistency:** calm, emotionally intelligent, fair, level-headed.

✔ **Supportive:** prepared to listen, make sure people are given the best chance to succeed, empathetic.

Chapter 14

✔ **Understanding the numbers:** leaders need to be finance-savvy and to have a grasp of the key metrics to be able to succeed.

✔ **Communicator:** confident and articulate, able to make the complex simple, so that everyone understands. 'Gets' the power of communication and the need to exploit it to the max.

✔ **Smart:** you don't need to have a PhD, but you do need to be competent, credible and able to assimilate large amounts of very varied information. Leaders need to understand the numbers, on top of everything else.

✔ **Positivity:** if the leaders aren't keeping people 'up there', who will? And they handle bad news in a way that makes people feel they're in safe hands. Great leaders see the opportunities and take them.

✔ **Character:** there's no exact leadership type, though most have charisma, are aspirational and inspirational, being able to inspire people to deliver to their best.

✔ **Standards:** no one wants to work for a crappy organisation producing poor work. The leader is the custodian of quality and therefore must constantly display high personal standards to remain credible.

✔ **Talent spotting:** great leaders recruit great people and put together fantastic teams, embracing the fact that in some ways they're more talented than the leader him/herself. They make sure people are aware of strengths and development needs so together they are strong.

✔ **Self-deprecation:** great leaders share minor weaknesses, which gives them credibility, humility and increases likeability.

✔ **Revel in diversity:** leaders know their own strengths and those of the people around them and know that difference is stronger than sameness.

And my favourite:

✔ **Hard empathy:** the ability to make people feel important, valued and valuable; to know exactly where they fit and what's required; to feel vital to the success of the organisation; challenged yet appreciated and recognised for their contribution. Imagine – who wouldn't want to work for someone like that?!

> Great leaders know they can't always choose what happens, but they can always choose their own responses.

Developing leaders is a lifelong process and something we believe the leader or potential leader should take their own responsibility for. Yes, you can go off to Harvard or Tsinghua or the LSE, and that's all great stuff, but not everyone has that opportunity and anyway, we believe it's only half the story.

We're massive fans of mentoring. Anyone who's serious about their leadership career should find themselves a mentor, someone who's an inspirational leader (the good guys are usually happy to give some time to promote good leadership in others). People have so much experience and knowledge, yet some go to the grave without passing it on – tragic. Coaching is also a great tool. While this requires more investment, the returns are great. Buying in trained professionals or running coaching programmes in-house are highly recommended.

Other great methods of providing low-cost leadership development include:

● In-house and/or externally facilitated leadership programmes linked to work-based projects

● Job swaps, work shadowing, visits

● Projects and self-study

● e-learning, distance learning

● Chairing meetings, working parties and committees

● Non-executive directorships/trusteeships – paid and unpaid

The most important thing is that leaders in the making must have access to this development on the way up – once they're there it's too late:

Francis is a brilliant IT programmer. I mean really fantastic; his work has made his organisation a lot of profit, people like him, he's a cool guy. He'd never really thought about being a leader and since his work–life balance was so important, he watched others take on the hassle and responsibility with a thankful thought that it wasn't him. However, his bosses identified Francis as the next leadership candidate. Between them they persuaded him into a promotion he didn't really feel confident about. OK, so the money would come in handy and Francis was flattered he was so well thought of, so he agreed to give it a go. To cut a long story short, he bombed, in a big way. He didn't possess the leadership skills to inspire and engage the team. He didn't know how to be a leader. Morale and productivity fell, a couple of key people left and Francis ended up on the verge of a nervous breakdown.

Grow your own leaders:

- Work out how leadership works within your organisation

- Recruit potential leaders – you can test this at interview and check aspirations

- Start developing them and imparting knowledge from day one, always managing expectations

- Have robust talent management in place so succession planning is always up to date and you can identify future leaders (see Chapter 13)

Discuss how leadership works within your organisation with existing leaders at all levels and agree on the essential components that will make up your style – a 'leadership charter' if you like. If everyone's aligned there's still room for individual style but there will be much less conflict and ambiguity, and more consistency. This is a very good thing. You could even bring in a facilitator to help you do this.

- Provide internal challenges and projects to test ability and inspire

- Use external secondments and experiential learning to keep things fresh

- Check aspirations, development plans and personal circumstances regularly – things change

- Measure and manage progress, giving lots of feedback

- Appoint fairly

If you only do three things:

1
Create great leaders at all levels, understanding the impact of getting it right

2
Develop the leaders of the future on the way up, always managing aspirations

3
Invest in a mentoring scheme with trained mentors and/or find a mentor for yourself

15

Getting stuff done

Most successful people set goals for themselves, write them down and think about what it will be like once they're there. It's the same with successful organisations. Sometimes, though, they go into planning overkill and spend so much time building strategy, budgets and KPIs and then beating their people into submission to deliver on the nail that they miss opportunities. We believe there's a happy medium.

From a big picture point of view it's important to know where you're going – you wouldn't set off on holiday without knowing where you were heading and more or less how you were getting there – unless you're a true free spirit and have the time and resources available to be able to experiment.

> It's a cliché, but if you fail to plan you plan to fail.

If you are one of the lucky ones who does have plenty of cash and/or low overheads then you can probably try stuff out and see if it works (not ideal to be honest!). However, the majority of us are not in this situation and therefore need a plan.

The world moves fast, and information flow is super rapid. This makes having an accurate five-year strategic plan and three years' budget and cashflow projections almost impossible. Our take on this is to have strong strategic intent, work out the non-negotiables in terms of achievement, vision, mission and values. Then be flexible about the detail and prepare to veer off plan if the situation dictates. This way you'll be able to pick up the opportunities without getting too distracted or moving too far away from your strategic goals.

A goal

- What you want
- How you'll get there
- Actions (in manageable chunks)
- When
- How will you know
- Measure and evaluate

Goals and objectives must be:

- **Aligned to the big picture:** so people know they are contributing to the greater vision

- **Understood:** many people don't know or understand their targets and goals; communication is key

- **Self-generated:** where possible, people are far more motivated to achieve goals they came up with themselves

- **Inspiring:** people are more likely to push to achieve something exciting

- **Monitored:** so that people know how they, their team and the organisation are doing

- **SMARTER** (see box opposite)

SMARTER is nothing new, but it does work.

Specific: we'll sell 50 houses.

Measurable: sales need to increase by 25% year on year.

Achievable: realistic; becoming the biggest property developer in the world within the next year isn't likely if you're currently running a handyman service.

Relevant: within the remit and capabilities of individual, team and organisation.

Timed: we'll deliver your extension by 31 December.

Engaging: if we do this it will put us over budget next month

Reviewed: we'll review at the end of May to ensure we're on target.

> A couple of years ago we built an online talent management system for a large, well-known organisation. This included a section for setting, measuring and reporting on goals and objectives. As part of the project, existing goals were to be uploaded into our system from spreadsheets provided by the client so that people could go right in and start to report. We discovered four things:
>
> 1. Not everyone's goals had been written down.
>
> 2. Many people hadn't been set any goals (even though head office were confident that everyone knew and were working towards them).
>
> 3. In quite a lot of cases, the goals people were working to were completely different from the goals the company had recorded.
>
> 4. In some cases, people had 20 or more personal objectives, which is unmanageable.

Unfortunately the boxed situation above is pretty common – have you checked lately that everyone in your organisation knows what they're supposed to be focusing on?

Things don't go off track because people are bad or hopeless. It's usually because organisations make the goals so complex that impact is lost in the confusion and there is no way of monitoring and measuring progress (which in turn is demotivating).

Inspiring goals come from:

- A great vision and values that people can be proud of

- A sense of direction and purpose

- Understanding the impact their contribution brings

- Ownership – individual and team spirit

- Clarity – make it simple

- Activities people can relate to and become excited about

- Easy ways to know how they're doing

- Knowing what it'll be like once they've got there

Once people are feeling pretty pepped up and ready to get started, there are a few things they'll need to do to 'make things happen':

- Prioritise – think about:

  ○ Urgent and/or important

  ○ Short, medium, long term

  ○ Hard, medium, easy

  ○ Resource required

  ○ Quick wins (easy, short term, little resource) and go from there

- Chunk down (you can try to cram a whole slab of toffee into your mouth or you can break it into manageable chunks – it's the same with goals and tasks)

- Set deadlines (always under-promise and over-deliver)

- Organise resources

The power of visualisation

This isn't weirdy stuff – it works because it's all about self-belief. Athletes do it, top presenters do it, you and your teams can do it with your goals. Skilled leaders paint the picture of success so that people are experiencing it before they even get there. Try it next time you have a presentation to deliver. Close your eyes (maybe when you're drifting off to sleep at night) and visualise the situation you're going into. Imagine it going well, people smiling, clapping, nodding. Then keep doing it every time you're in planning mode for the presentation or whenever you think about it, right up to the actual event. By the time you get to it you'll feel calmer and more confident. This will make you perform better. It's the same with goals.

● Then, in the words of Nike, 'Just do it' – all the planning and strategising in the world is a complete waste of time unless there's some action.

Learn to think 'urgent/important' about everything you do – use the diagram below to help you.

Sometimes it's easier or more fun to do the stuff in the bottom left box – bad move. Be disciplined and play the BANJOE instead (Bang A Nasty Job Off Early)!

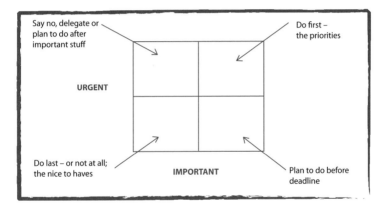

Time management

There are lots of techniques for managing time and some of these are listed below. By far the most important factor, though – and it sounds boring – is self-discipline. Personal focus, drive and organisation make a world of difference when it comes to achievement. So that's the place to start.

10 top time tips:

1. Have a constant eye on the goals, priorities and outcomes

2. Brain dump – get everything out of your head and on to a list or into a diary or calendar

3. Ban bits of paper and invest in a PDA or notebook that can easily be carried round

4. Write everything down

5. Plan using the urgent vs. important grid on the previous page

6. Break big tasks down into manageable chunks so it's easy to get started

7. Stop procrastinating and make 'energy' and 'action' your buzzwords

8. Be assertive about saying no and preventing interruptions

9. Ask for help

10. Manage expectations (always under-promise and over-deliver)

Bonus tip: manage yourself and the time stuff will follow.

There's a useful story that does the rounds, which perfectly illustrates the need to prioritise. Here's an abridged version.

A professor stands in front of his class holding a glass jar, which he fills to the top with large rocks. He asks the students, 'Is the jar full yet?', to which most of the students reply 'Yes'.

Then he adds smaller rocks to the jar. He asks again and again they answer in the affirmative. He goes on to add sand, which fills the gaps, again asks the question, to which most people say 'Yes'. Last he adds water, which finally fills the jar.

If the sand and small rocks had gone in first, he never would have fitted in any larger rocks. This shows that you need to make time to get the big important stuff done or all the small stuff (generally, reactive tasks) will get in the way.

Delegation

You know those stressed-out managers who always have too much to do but the success of an operation depends on them? They're the ones who don't delegate. Delegation is where one person divests responsibility and authority for a task to another. The reverse of delegation is micro-management. At learnpurple we detest micro-management.

> One man's boring task is another man's stimulating challenge

Managers sometimes don't delegate because they believe they can do it better themselves; or they don't want to 'lose control'; or it's just too much work to stop and explain and then support someone else to do the task. This means they miss out on a massive opportunity to: (a) win themselves more time; (b) develop others; (c) provide motivation; (d) build trust; (e) assist succession planning. I could go on . . .

Delegation should be:

- A two-way 'contract'
- Properly explained – and understanding checked
- Properly resourced and supported
- Safe and without undue risk (you can build up levels of complexity and difficulty as you progress and as people become more confident)
- Monitored but not interfered with
- SMARTER (which adds 'Engaged' and 'Reviewed' to SMART)

Quick guide to delegation:

- Define the task or responsibility to be undertaken
- Decide who's the best person for the job (or, better still, ask the team to decide)
- Explain the 'Why' (very important)
- Agree what a good result looks like

- Agree resources to be made available

- Agree deadline and milestones

- Agree how reporting back will work

- Provide support

- Leave well alone

- Review

- Feedback

- Celebrate (as appropriate to the task and result)

- Say thank you

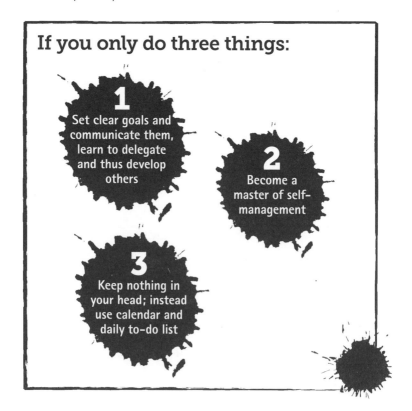

If you only do three things:

1
Set clear goals and communicate them, learn to delegate and thus develop others

2
Become a master of self-management

3
Keep nothing in your head; instead use calendar and daily to-do list

16

Team dynamics and having fun

I t stands to reason that if people feel happy and are enjoying their work they'll be more motivated and productive and therefore perform well and achieve better results for the organisation. Obviously all the stuff from Chapter 15 about goals has also got to be in place for a team to perform well. You also want to ensure that your people work well as a team and so this chapter is all about individuals working cohesively together.

> The obvious thing to do is to employ nice people who will get on with those around them and fit into your culture. Think about building some fun into work life – see the second half of this chapter. At learnpurple, we include 'fun' as one of our values.

For teams to work well together it's first important that people understand one another's motivations – what makes a person 'tick'. They'll feel more committed to the organisation and team, and communication will be better.

The fast-track way to understanding team dynamics is to use psychometrics. We use tools called iWAM® and SDI®, but there are plenty out there – use a search engine to find them.

You know the first few months of a person joining? When people are trying to figure them out? Well, if you use psychometrics you can find a shortcut through the process, which minimises possible conflict and enables people to settle in and become productive much quicker. If you've used psychometrics during the selection, the next steps would be:

> If you can't run to the use of psychometrics (it really is well worth finding an expert to help you), have honest conversations with new people about how best they'd like to be managed and encourage everyone to be honest and straightforward about their own personality traits. Once you make this part of your culture, it makes for a very progressive environment.

1. Give the new starter feedback.

2. Gain their permission to share their results along with those of others in their team.

3. Hold a group session to discuss similarities and differences together with roles and responsibilities, goals, etc. – maybe at the next team meeting. We recommend doing this once a year – you can make it a fun session as well as a very important and informative one.

If people have a full understanding of what drives themselves and their colleagues it legitimises feedback at this level, and provides a transparency that's a perfect basis for solving issues and complex challenges.

> I was once on a conference line-up with an extremely senior and pretty hard-nosed person who headed up mergers and acquisitions for a well-known corporation. At question time someone asked him how he'd know whether he'd be able to work well with an existing leadership team. He said he wouldn't consider moving forward unless he'd put them all through psychometric tests. This isn't 'mumbo jumbo fluffy HR stuff' – it's great business sense.

People are going to work better if they like each other. This isn't about 'cloning people' – diversity is definitely something that will enhance your organisation. If you look back at the Citizen M recruitment method (see Chapter 5), what they're doing there is observing the candidates throughout the assessment process. The key thing they're looking for is whether the people are sociable and fun who are likely to get on with each other and with their guests.

Recruit for attitude and train for skill.

The flatter the structure and the more trust and respect you engender, the more likely it is that people will be able to feel relaxed and enjoy themselves at work. This is a major contributor to positive team dynamics. You might feel that this is stating the obvious. Sadly, however, there are still so many officious manager types at large that it has to be mentioned. If you have a deeply hierarchical structure complete with inherent blame culture, and little trust or respect, it is almost impossible to engage and retain people and have them working positively and productively in teams.

It might be that you feel this is working for you at the moment. However, if you read Chapter 20 you'll see why that might not be the case for much longer.

Team dynamics are also seriously enhanced by having fun. If you work it out, people spend about 100,000 hours at work during their lives, so it stands to reason they should be enjoying them. You don't want to turn the place into a comedy club, though, so balance is key – 'work hard, play hard'.

Making mistakes

My mum used to say, 'The person who never made a mistake never made anything' – it turns out she was paraphrasing Einstein. If people feel it's OK to get something wrong as long as they learn something from the experience, you will create an organisation where creativity and innovation are encouraged. The sort of stimulating environment where people are learning all the time, don't spend time making excuses or trying to cover up stuff and no one feels scared of the consequences of getting something wrong. There is one caveat, though: people shouldn't keep making the same mistake. If this is the case, there's a development need, something lacking in the resources or system, or they're in the wrong role.

At learnpurple, if people are apprehensive about trying something new or tricky, our mantra is 'Just do it: what's the worst that can happen?' Once you get that inside your head and know you'll be supported through, it becomes easy to take action. Try it – you might like it. Obviously this doesn't apply if you're working in the medical profession, in a nuclear power plant or other hazardous environment . . .

Celebrating mistakes is seriously enhanced if leadership can be self-deprecating from time to time and admit a few 'dropped balls'. Some organisations have a 'mistake of the month' session when they swap stories, voting for the most outrageous error.

Dyson

Entrepreneur inventor Sir James Dyson says this:

'I made 5,127 prototypes of my vacuum before I got it right. There were 5,126 failures. But I learned from each one. That's how I came up with a solution. So I don't mind failure. I've always thought that schoolchildren should be marked by the number of failures they've had. The child who tries strange things and experiences lots of failures to get there is probably more creative... We're taught to do things the right way. But if you want to discover something that other people haven't, you need to do things the wrong way. Initiate a failure by doing something that's very silly, unthinkable, naughty, dangerous. Watching why that fails can take you on a completely different path. It's exciting, actually.'

Source: Fast Company (www.fastcompany.com)

Here are a few suggestions for enhancing fun at work that we've experienced or seen in action (so we know they work):

- Have lunch together

- Tell stories

- Use humour (appropriately – pointing at your PowerPoint presentation with a banana is not, in the majority of workplaces, appropriate)

- Manage time (see Chapter 12) so there's less stress and more time for fun

- Share books and discuss them

- Learn a language (maybe someone on the team could teach the basics of their language?)

- Learn to dance together

- Sweepstakes for major sporting events such as the World Cup

- Have fun warm-up exercises for team meetings

- Get everyone to email round their top five achievements at the end of each week and introduce a fun element

- Don't take stuff too seriously

- Introduce a fun budget for treats or activities (to be managed by the team, not the manager)

- Have a company or team trip (we had a **lot** of fun when we all went to Ibiza!) – this gives lasting memories and becomes part of the organisation 'story book'

- Make a TV screen available for major events and sporting fixtures (this stops people going off sick to watch and is a bonding exercise which, in our view, is worth a couple of hours' down time)

- Talk about top five films, songs, etc.

- Brighten up the environment

- Put up an employee photo board

What fun at work should not be:

Exclusive

Racist, sexist, or any other 'ist'

Sarcastic

Interfering with work and/or goals

Intrusive (although we love fun, we don't love those round robin emails people send)

Damaging to the reputation of an individual, team or organisation

Around sensitive issues

And remember: everyone's different, so keep it mature and sensible, making sure the fun is never going to offend anyone.

- Organise birthday celebrations

- Present awards, spoof awards (e.g. at Christmas)

- Provide food at meetings (but keep it healthy!)

- Organise social events, e.g. summer picnic

- Arrange after-work events such as bowling, ice skating or theatre trips

If you only do three things:

1 Make sure people understand what drives themselves and their colleagues (use psychometrics)

2 Be big on trust and celebrate mistakes

3 Be creative – have some fun!

17

Attitude, skills and knowledge

So you have the right people in the right roles and responsibilities. They fit your culture, are trusted, interested and inspired, receive feedback, have fun and are thanked for their contribution. But they still need the tools to do the job and a big part of this includes having the right:

- Attitude

- Skills

- Knowledge

Some of this will be down to good communication and knowing where to go to find the information they need. However, there may still need to be some input from the organisation to fully equip people to be able to perform well.

Attitude

If the circumstances are right (see above and the previous chapters of this book), attitude is absolutely the responsibility of the individual. You'd do worse than to make this clear at interview and again during the induction. The message is along the lines of: 'We want you to do well here and enjoy being part of our team. If, however, at any time you feel negative or something is preventing you from fulfilling your commitment to us, it's your responsibility to come and talk to one of us so that we can help you resolve it as soon as possible'.

> We'd suggest operating a 'zero-tolerance policy' when it comes to negativity. Because one disengaged person with a poor attitude can cause a lot of damage. At best they are being unproductive, at worst they are sabotaging your workplace.

You need to trust your instinct here and be aware of any unresolved conflict and/or observe any negative body language. This includes lack of eye contact; mumbling and grumbling; poor posture (stooped shoulders); frowning; lack of concentration on what's been said; looking bored.

Come on, you don't have to be a body language expert to know. **Quite often, though, people choose to ignore negative body language because they don't want to confront it.** This is where assertiveness, support and empathy come in, as well as believing that people are basically good and want to do well.

Be aware that people take in information in different ways; they even listen in different ways. Someone might look distracted when really they are thinking about what's been said. Some would rather read an instruction than be told orally.

If the person with the less than positive attitude hasn't raised it with someone, then the line manager is responsible for tackling it. It's not necessary to make a big deal out of this though; the point is (in the spirit of trust and openness) to hold an empathetic, exploratory conversation. It may be that as soon as you raise the issue, the person opens up to you. Or there might need to be more input and examples given. Either way, it's important to keep going until resolution or an action plan has been put in place.

> Giving people a trained buddy or mentor is a good way to ensure negativity is dealt with quickly and outside the management structure (generally the best way for all).

Issues are easily resolved the majority of the time. It might be a personal issue requiring some support or time off. It might be that someone doesn't have the support they need. They might be in the wrong role. The important thing is to probe, listen and resolve as soon as possible.

Skills and knowledge

You'll be covering the basics during the induction period. This might be achieved through one-to-one work with a colleague or through more formal means. The important thing is to avoid 'sheep-dipping' people through the same skills-based learning. A far better approach is to audit skills against the requirements of the role and then draw up a development plan for each individual. Then make it their responsibility to complete the plan. This is very important.

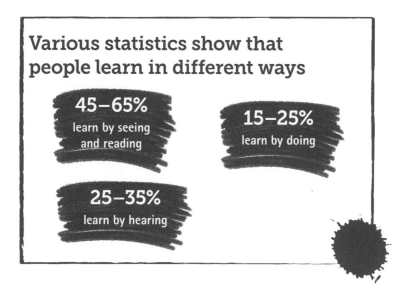

Various statistics show that people learn in different ways

45–65%
learn by seeing and reading

15–25%
learn by doing

25–35%
learn by hearing

This is why traditional 'chalk and talk' methods aren't particularly effective.

You'll need to make sure resources are available, but in my view the days of managers chasing people around to attend courses are long gone. The review process must be in place to monitor progress (and as mentioned in Chapter 13, if you can automate this, it's a whole lot easier to manage).

People learn in different ways, therefore learning plans have to be different.

If they are attending classroom sessions, a mix of learning styles will need to be provided for. If they are learning on an individual basis the great thing is that you can vary the ways they learn. Here are some options – as you will see, many of these are low-cost, or no-cost and may therefore be preferable to traditional learning and development courses when it comes to skills transfer:

- Reading books and journals (we love in-house learning libraries)

- Textbooks and technical guides

- Internet search – there's loads of free stuff out there

Chapter 17

- Podcasts

- Webcasts

- E-learning

- Distance learning

- In-house guides and other learning resources

- Professional bodies' fact sheets

- Job swaps

- Secondments

- Work shadowing

- Projects

- Experiences such as competitor visits

- Interviewing colleagues

- Coaching

- Mentoring (a fantastic and definitely under-exploited way to learn)

> Trainers must be expert enough to be able to draw from a 'toolbox' of: theory; exercises; real-life, relevant stories and examples; case studies; and so forth. This is why not just anyone can pick up a trainer's notes and/or a presentation and deliver it – to achieve the desired results they have to really know what they are doing.

One-to-group development still has a very important role to play. It's brilliant for leadership development or for specific subjects such as customer service or sales – where participants can learn from one another as well as the expert trainer. It's vital though that learning is participant-led. Meaning that the trainer is interacting with the learners at the start of the session or beforehand to find out a number of things about the topic they'll be learning about:

- What they know already

- What their experiences are

- How they'd rate their competency

- How it works for them within their role

- What they'd like to improve

- Any specifics they'd like to cover

The trainer then facilitates a session, which draws upon:

- His or her own knowledge of the subject

- The knowledge and experiences of the group

Then puts them together (see box on the next page) to provide a stimulating and interactive session, which will allow people to see, hear and do.

Whatever the delivery method, learning should be:

- Appropriate to the individual

- Appropriate to the role

- Planned

- Discussed beforehand to agree goals and outcomes

- Well executed

- Reviewed, and outcomes checked both after the learning and again after three/six months

People often ask us how best to utilise a limited learning and development budget. Obviously it will depend on the circumstances, but generally we'd say that developing middle management is key. This is because, to the people below them, they 'are' the organisation. They have a big influence on and responsibility for communication and how progress is made. Customer service training also brings a very quick return on investment

Soho House Group

Soho House Group invested in a modular leadership programme. This consisted of 12 half-day facilitated modules plus some sessions in smaller groups using coaching techniques to accommodate the wide range of styles and needs of the participants. The learning was tailored for each group and real-life examples and case studies were used. This style of participant-led learning is the way to go. At the beginning of each session there was a facilitated discussion along the lines of:

- *What do you already know about this subject?*

- *What have your experiences been?*

- *What goes well?*

- *And not so well?*

- *What would you like to fix?*

- *What would you like to share with others?*

And so on ... This way the facilitator can reach into his or her 'bag of tricks' for the required mix of theory, exercises, case studies and examples, as well as setting follow-up work to be done in between sessions to underpin the learning.

So much more effective than churning out the same old PowerPoint presentation ...

If you only do three things:

1 Deal with negativity fast, firmly, yet with empathy

2 Use learning that's appropriate to the individual

3 Optimise the use of the best of low-cost/ no-cost methods backed up with experts in the classroom for certain topics

18

Managing aspirations and succession

Managing aspirations and succession

As you will know by now, if you can successfully engage and retain good people your organisation will be more profitable. But by how much? Few people measure the cost of attrition, i.e. how much is swiped off the bottom line every time a person leaves. This is probably because it's just too terrifying a figure. When we talk to business leaders about this, quite often they say, 'It's just the way things are, it's a fact of corporate life, a cost of doing business' and have little or no aspiration to make business improvements in this area. This is pure madness.

OK, it wouldn't be healthy to retain everyone, but it just doesn't make sense that, in our wide experience of helping businesses to reduce labour turnover, many service organisations lose upwards of 30% of their people each year. What a waste.

There's lots of research about how much it costs when a person leaves, for example a study a few years ago from EP First/Saratoga concluded that if a manager leaves it will cost five times their salary package; and up to 10 times for a director. Now that is terrifying. This is why it can cost so much:

Direct costs:

- Recruitment
- Management time
- Interim/temp cover
- Development

Indirect costs:

- Disruption to the business
- Reduced productivity
- Lost opportunities/revenue
- Knowledge loss
- Customer relationships
- Reputation
- Motivation and morale
- Quality
- Continuity
- Increased competitor threat
- Knock-on attrition

When people do measure attrition costs they tend to look at the direct costs but ignore the very significant indirect costs. Suppose one of your top sales managers left to go to a competitor. Some of her customers and members of the team follow and the people left behind are feeling displaced. Their new manager doesn't arrive for six months – you can see how profits would suffer.

Our research shows that if people's aspirations were met, 70% of those who leave an organisation would stay. That's pretty major stuff and a compelling reason to sort this out.

> The amount of activity and resource allocated to recruitment is rarely mirrored when it comes to engagement and retention. Some companies think little of spending £500,000 on recruitment over a year yet don't put 10% of this figure towards keeping people.

All the advice in this book will help with retaining your talent. But there are some specific things you could do to help this happen. Regularly reviewing employees' progress and finding out what their aspirations are makes sense. If it suits the business, it's important to ensure these aspirations are fulfilled. Be aware that not all talented people want promotion – find out what they do want. It makes sense to review frequently as change can be rapid. If you can automate this, the data is faster, easier, more up-to-date and more accessible.

Also recommended is the use of succession and business planning techniques to identify:

- Roles likely to be created or freed up in the future
- Who is aspiring to change
- What it will take to get them job-ready
- Who is ready to take on a job
- Who is overdue a move
- Who is at risk of leaving

● Who should be managed out of their role or out of the business (sorry, but it has to be said: if, despite all the circumstances and support being right, someone is disengaged and not contributing, they need to be helped up or managed out before they have a detrimental effect on others)

Malmaison and Hotel du Vin Group

When Robert Cook, CEO of the company that owns the Malmaison and Hotel du Vin groups, introduced an online system for managing the progress and aspirations of their 2,500 people, the company saved over £500,000 per annum.

● *Labour turnover dramatically reduced to 30% (industry average is 65%), saving at the most conservative estimate £270,000.*

● *Targeted and timely learning and development saved over £10,000.*

● *Recruitment costs halved, saving the group approximately £125,000 p.a.*

● *New properties are 80% staffed from within, with clear development plans, thanks to robust succession and training needs analysis.*

People have a right to know where they are going

They want to know when and how they will get there and how they could be affected. An effective way to do this is through regular appraisals and reviews (see Chapter 13).

When we first started, for example, we found out that on average, 85% of employees in the hospitality industry did not have a regular appraisal. Over the last 10 years we've discovered that many other industries don't fare much better and that the solutions we designed for the fabulous though challenging hospitality industry work everywhere else.

Setting up an effective two-way communication system enabling people to share their aspirations gives a head start on competitors and may well uncover people with talents and ambition who would otherwise not be identified. Time and work pressures can make it difficult for managers to undertake appraisals, but for all of the reasons cited, it is important not to neglect them.

When managing aspirations

- Be realistic

- Encourage people to drive their own progress

- Make strategic plans – avoid panic recruiting

It's important to remember that employees are individuals with their own wants and needs. Whilst we're not generally 'box' people, we find this nine-box grid (see below) rather useful for succession planning and the talent review.

This tool helps map people according to their performance scores and their potential ratings for the following 12 months. You can't just pluck these ratings out of thin air. There has to be a fair and consistent way of measuring them. The version we use will result in the following differentiators. On the following pages is a definition of each and a guide of what the next steps are to engage, develop and retain these individuals and how future leaders are identified.

Many organisations find succession planning too detailed and difficult to do. In our view, it's an absolute no-brainer to automate it and encourage employees to drive their own progress via a consistent, effective and efficient channel. And it makes utilising a nine-box grid (below) simple, fair and consistent.

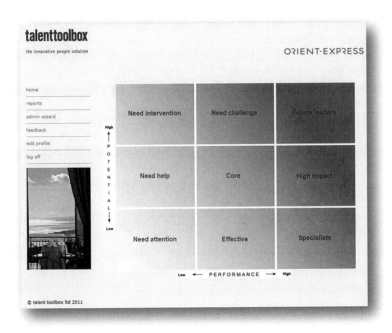

Box 1: Need Attention

Definition: These employees are showing low potential and also low performance. They under-perform and aren't currently showing any scope for improvement. They are likely to be disengaged: at best they are adding little and at worst could be sabotaging the organisation and causing others to feel demotivated.

Actions: Here management has to take a tough decision: either challenging them to improve their performance; or taking action which may ultimately move them on.

Box 2: Need Help

Definition: These employees have average potential but show low performance. This could be due to disengagement; moving too

soon; inadequate induction or development; not coping with manager, colleagues, change or culture.

Actions: They have the potential to perform better if given the opportunity, motivation, support and perhaps development.

Box 3: Need Intervention

Definition: These are employees who have a lot of potential but simply aren't performing. They are a wasted resource and intervention is needed to find out why they fall into this category. They are either in the wrong role, wrong organisation/culture or not responding to their current team or manager (who has failed to harness their potential), or they have other issues that, for the good of the employee and the organisation, need to be explored.

Actions: A 'heart-to-heart' between the employee and a third party (and possibly with the line manager too) is required.

Box 4: Effective

Definition: These are employees with specific talents as they show higher performance when compared to their potential. They may have reached their full career potential so need recognition for their contribution together with effort around keeping them engaged, focused and motivated to get the desired results.

Actions: They may require personal development or progression via a project that might not be directly related to the role or the organisation.

Box 5: Core

Definition: These employees perform just up to the potential of the role though they may be capable of out-performing if given the required motivation or challenge.

Actions: If they are 'coasting' it is worth exploring why, e.g. disengagement; lack of challenge in role; unchallenged or demotivated by job content, team, change or culture. If they are happy in their role and performing consistently at this level, continue to engage them and celebrate their loyalty.

Box 6: Need Challenge

Definition: This category comprises employees who constantly show high potential but their performance is not up to that standard. They may not have sufficient motivation or inspiration to move forward. The organisation should recognise the value of this talent and work out how to obtain the best from every employee.

Actions: These employees can become great assets for the organisation, though they need to be kept challenged and receive recognition as they achieve their goals. To increase performance levels, ensure they have the confidence, tools and freedom to achieve.

Box 7: Specialists

Definition: These are trusted professionals who perform at much higher levels than their potential because of some special talent they have. They could be people who for reasons of work–life balance or other circumstances have taken a less senior or complex role. Or they are very engaged and prepared to trade off challenge against the ability to stay within your organisation

Actions: They should be valued and efforts made to retain them by rewarding and recognising them. If possible allow them to pass on their skills and experience through mentoring other high performers/potentials.

Box 8: High Impact

Definition: These are performers who with grooming, direction, development and/or motivation can become the future leaders. They may have lost motivation, direction or pace with the changes in the organisation. They are similar to the 'need help' and 'core' employees, but they can be among the top talent.

Actions: The organisation needs to ensure they keep engaged, motivated and challenged and that they receive recognition for their contribution.

Box 9: Future Leaders

Definition: These employees are the leaders of the near future and are the current best possible options for succession at senior positions. They demonstrate leadership qualities and produce results. They have influence and people look up to them and seek their advice. They get the job done and have broad experience and knowledge.

Actions: They need to be nurtured and every effort made to challenge and engage them. They also need to be rewarded appropriately. They will need to progress (personally and within the organisation), so ensure that there are opportunities to grow through promotion or other high-profile challenges. If there are no opportunities available it may be advisable to help them find a secondment or a new challenge in a non-competing organisation, leaving the door open for a future return.

If you only do three things:

1
Focus the mind by working out how much people leaving actually costs your organisation every year (there's a free online calculator at www.purpleyour people.com)

2
Regularly review employee progress and aspirations

3
Find a way to make succession planning work for you

19

Wellbeing:
healthy = productive =
profitable

Being healthy and happy at work is not a fuzzy notion. There are definite bottom-line benefits such as good levels of employee engagement and retention, high motivation and productivity, employee satisfaction, creativity and innovation, reduced absenteeism and less time lost on dealing with conflict.

Assuming you have all the statutory health and safety requirements fully up to date (and if you haven't, put down this book and do something about it straight away), a physically and mentally healthy culture is likely to include all or some of the following:

- General focus on wellbeing

- Equality

- Support and empathy

- Respect

- Trust

- Shared values

- Consultation

- Fair treatment

- Positive environment

- A safe and well-run place to work

- Good leadership

- Attendance culture

- Healthy CSR (see box opposite)

CSR (corporate social responsibility) is a key part of becoming a great place to work. CSR means taking positive action towards aligning your values and the way you do things with the needs of everyone your organisation can have an impact on. This encompasses the business owners and investors, employees and customers, but also suppliers and other partners, the community, other specific groups, the environment and society as a whole.

With team members who are able to:

- Drive their own progress

- Feel in control over their own role

- Benefit society

- Fulfill both personal and work goals

- Be healthy and energetic

- Understand how they fit into the big picture

You can see how more or less everything in this book would make a positive contribution to wellbeing at work. However, there are a few specifics you should know.

How to create a wellbeing culture

All of the previously mentioned points are big, important areas and you should be working towards them anyway. But there are a few little (relatively low-investment) things you could do immediately which will give out a strong message: we care about the people we work with and their wellbeing. These could include:

- Providing a pleasant working environment

- Making healthy drinks and plenty of water available

- Free fruit and healthy snacks

> The behaviours of managers, leaders, employees, the organisation as a whole all need to show that they're really on board with a 'wellbeing' culture or you may as well not make the effort in the first place. Leaders and managers have to 'walk the talk'.

Wellbeing: healthy = productive = profitable

- Quiet room/chill-out zone

- Room for chatting and taking breaks

- Allow use of headphones for people who are focusing on work in a noisy environment (or use 'do not disturb' signals such as flags)

- Make sure people take proper breaks and all of their holiday entitlement

- Encourage exercise (even if it's just a walk round the block)

- Subsidised gym membership

- In-chair office massage

- Time management sessions to help people control their workload

- Nutrition workshops

- Good supportive chairs

- Workplace assessment

- Buddy or employee counsellor

- Random acts of kindness

eBay (UK)

'We introduced energiseYou On-Site Chair Massage as a new employee benefit to help improve employee wellbeing. Everyone at eBay works hard and spends most of their time at a computer. At eBay the service has made an excellent impact on reducing workplace stress and keeping morale and motivation high. Staff love it!'

Best of all, ask your employees what would make your organisation a better place to work.

Work–life balance (WLB)

WLB is not just about being 'family friendly'. It's about balancing the needs of the organisation and the individual in order to accommodate the responsibilities and aspirations of your employee – which, in our view, is a business imperative. As with all of this stuff, WLB benefits the bottom line. Nowadays, people demand it and great places to work offer it. So if you're not providing a good WLB already, you are going to need to.

Tom commutes 90 minutes each way to his job in the City. He recently became a father for the first time and is keen to support his wife and also to spend time with Daisy, his new daughter, watching her grow. Tom's employer allowed him to change his working arrangements so he could spend a day a week working at home and then come into the office early and leave earlier on the other days. In his last appraisal, Tom wrote:

'I really appreciate the flexibility you've given me. It makes such a difference to my life. I still achieve what I did before but I get to put Daisy to bed every night and I feel less stressed than I thought I'd be as a new Dad.'

Makes sense, really, doesn't it?

It's a shameless generalisation, but Generation Y (see Chapter 20) tends to place WLB high on their list of priorities. Chat with a few graduates and you'll see what I mean.

It might be that you'll experience some resistance from the 'old school' (and by that I mean old in attitude, not necessarily age). If you search the internet you'll find plenty of case studies evidencing the positive benefits of WLB which can be used to make your case.

In brief, a 10-point plan for implementing better WLB is:

1. Identify and understand organisation and employee needs and aspirations

2. Work out what your policies on WLB will be

3. Engage leadership team and managers

4. Build a supportive environment

5. Communicate the new arrangements

6. Run a pilot and evaluate

7. Assess

8. Amend and refine

9. Communicate to all

10. Monitor, evaluate, evolve.

Bonus tip: listen to your people, start simple and build

Stress

Put very simply, stress is an extreme form of excitement (although at the time it doesn't feel like this). You need a little excitement to feel motivated and energised. Too much, though, and bad things can happen – 'stressed-out' people can experience anxiety, apathy, depression, trouble sleeping, tiredness, irritability, lack of concentration, headaches, muscular problems, back pain, stomach issues, alcohol and drug abuse, heart disease and, in extreme cases, death. Stress is the number one reason for long-term sickness absence (Chartered Institute of Personnel and Development and Simplyhealth 2010) and a very real cause of disengagement.

Even if you're following the **'Purple Plan'** and are doing all the right things, it's natural that there might still be excessive stress on occasions.

In our experience this is often down to the individual. Sometimes people push themselves too hard, or allow others to pressure them. The single best thing you can do is to teach people that they are in control of their own behaviour and if they don't feel good they need to do something about it. They might need help with assertiveness, organisational skills or managing conflict to support them. The mantra for this is:

Remember (this one's worth repeating): you cannot always choose the events around you or other people's behaviour but you can always choose your own response.

Drugs and alcohol

Substance abuse is a fact of life and can cause severe issues at work if left unchecked, so here's a quick guide:

1. Introduce a robust but straightforward alcohol and drug abuse policy and publicise it well.

2. Make sure people know where to find support if they have an issue (and put some signs in lavatories and locker rooms so others don't notice people taking down helpline numbers).

3. Know how to spot abuse.

4. Make sure issues are dealt with swiftly; you owe it to the wellbeing of the workplace. It's not a good idea to go round accusing people of substance abuse, but you can manage poor work quality or behaviour, as described in Chapter 12, and try to uncover the root cause.

Symptoms include: poor quality of work, poor personal hygiene or appearance, deterioration of relationships, mood and behaviour changes, lethargy, unscheduled absence or breaks, lateness, anxiety and paranoia, lack of co-ordination, slurred speech, money problems, theft.

Any one or all of these could be due to something else entirely, such as depression or illness, so tread carefully.

5. Discuss and listen. Be empathetic and prepared to help; firm and fair.

6. Agree next steps and record them.

7. Monitor.

If things don't improve, you'll need to refer to your disciplinary policy or check with your legal adviser, a government guide (such as the UK Advisory, Conciliation and Arbitration Service (ACAS)) or your HR resource. If you're following the steps in Chapter 12 this will always be a last resort.

The last resort

If you don't have a disciplinary policy (and this should be stated in every employee's conditions of work), a reasonable scenario would be.

Explain that since you feel your unofficial and supportive discussions haven't resulted in the required performance improvements, there are some steps to take. If you've done a good job on the goal setting and monitoring, this should not be in dispute.

In brief, these steps are:

1. Let the employee know in advance of your intention to hold an official meeting to discuss the issues and that this meeting may result in disciplinary action. Give them an option to bring an independent observer (if you're smart, your conditions will state that this should be someone from within the organisation).

● Hold the meeting: summarise the situation with examples.

● Be supportive and give the employee plenty of opportunity to explain.

● Agree next steps with clear metrics and timescales (these must allow a reasonable amount of time for improvement).

● If disciplinary measures are deemed appropriate, record in writing as a 'verbal warning'.

● Measure and follow up as agreed, always providing support to give the person the best possible chance of recovery.

2. If the situation still does not improve, repeat, this time issuing an official written warning.

And still no improvement? Then it may be necessary to dismiss the employee, following your company policy or legal advice.

If you only do three things:

1 Care about your people and introduce some things that will enhance wellbeing

2 Work out how work–life balance can be achieved and make it happen

3 Support people through difficult times, be firm but fair and act fast when necessary

20

The generation game:
why it matters

Chapter 20

Generation theory is a subject that is sometimes contentious, but there is plenty of evidence and research to show that it's well-grounded and sound. Also it appears to contradict somewhat the purple 'treat people as individuals' philosophy.

So let's have a few caveats before getting into it:

- Everyone's different and we applaud and celebrate that

- There are always exceptions to the rule

- Used wisely, what you're about to read can be extremely useful but shouldn't be taken too literally

The point of this chapter is to explain some of the generational conflicts experienced in business today, to give you some tools and understanding to help deal with them and engage the new generation of employees. It's useful to know and can explain a lot ...

Here goes

Generation theory seeks to explain how individuals born within one generation (approximately a 20-year period) will have a different view of the world from those born in another. This is because each generation is shaped by different economic, environmental and social norms.

- **Baby boomers:** born 1945–1961 (during the post-World War II baby boom)

- **Generation X:** born 1962–1981

- **Generation Y:** born 1982–2001

> Because we're not being too serious, you could do it by music:
>
> - Baby boomer: if you bought your first piece of music on vinyl.
>
> - Generation X: tapes or maybe early CDs.
>
> - Generation Y: CDs and digital music, e.g. iTunes.

The generation game: why it matters

I've only included the generations currently found in today's workforce. There are different opinions about the exact dates for each generation, so I've used the ones we subscribe to. Don't worry too much about the dates, though; it's the difference in characteristics that are important.

Here's a made-up scenario that we used as a role play at a conference to illustrate the message (unfortunately sometimes it's not so far from the reality!):

The interview

David, a 53-year-old director, is interviewing candidates for his company's graduate scheme. Along comes Poppy, a 21-year-old.

David: So, Poppy, my last question is: why specifically are you applying for our graduate scheme?

Poppy: I think this is a place I could learn a lot and do well; I'm also hoping to meet some of those celebrities you seem to attract as clients and of course I'd love to travel and be part of the glamour.

David: Er, OK. Thank you. Now, before we finish, do you have any questions for me?

Poppy: I'd just like to let you know I'd have to finish by five p.m. every Wednesday to go to my Spanish lesson.

David: In my day we weren't allowed to just go off for personal stuff when we felt like it – work came first. Is there any flexibility on that? Because obviously the business comes first.

Poppy: Well, not really – I'm halfway through you see. Also would I need to work any weekends?

David: Well, as a graduate you'd be expected to do what it takes, as I did on the way up. Are you another one who's going to be overly concerned about work–life balance?

Poppy: Oh yes, work–life balance is very important. So if I work evenings and weekends what do I get in return?

David: Surely you must realise that working occasional weekends and long hours is just the way things are.

Poppy: Hmm, well, OK. So when could I expect a promotion and a salary increase and by how much would it go up?

David: The graduate salary is £22K and we'd just have to see how it goes after that depending on how well you perform.

Poppy: So how would that be measured and over what time scale exactly? I want to be in a management position by the end of my graduate programme.

David: Your line manager would decide, though you'd have to complete your two-year programme first.

Poppy: So there's no hope of an increase for two whole years. I think I could be ready much sooner than that. When do we sit down to discuss my development?

David: Let's get started first, eh?

Poppy: Well, could I have a mentor then, someone senior in the company to help me? And how can I develop myself so I progress more quickly?

David (reluctantly): You are forceful; though I suppose tenacity is a positive thing. In my day it took five years, so two years is like a fast-track option. I suppose we could look at a mentor, though that certainly didn't happen when I was on the way up, I did it all on my own merits ...

Poppy: Will I be able to make my own decisions then, and drive my own progress?

David (exasperated): We're almost out of time – do you have one last question?

Poppy: Yes, David, how did I do? Do you think you'll be sending me an offer?

David: We'll let you know. And, by the way, it's Mr Saunders.

Below is a useful summary of characteristics which will illustrate how conflict or potential distrust could occur.

Baby Boomer	Generation X	Generation Y
Live to work	Work to live	Work to fund lifestyle
Long hours and dedication	Do the necessary and go home	WLB, bored easily
Motivated by prestige, perks, status	Motivated by change, freedom, respect, outputs	Motivated by making a difference
Knowledge = power	'Show me what you know'	Ask many questions (Generation 'Why?')
Compliance, parent–child relationship with employer	Adult-to-adult relationships	Confidence to have adult-to-adult relationship
Know they've done a good job	Like regular feedback	Like immediate feedback
Make own decisions without consultation	Take direction and then get on with it	Need constant collaboration/direction
Like structure and hierarchy	Have disdain for authority and structure	Family values – require nurturing environment
Like control	Hate being micro-managed	Need help with problem-solving, like to share
Want to lead	Self-reliant, cynical	Don't want to lead
Resist change	Relish change	Flexible
Value experience	Assert individuality	Experience irrelevant
Competitive and resilient	Want to fix boomers' 'mistakes'	Take on tough, meaningful jobs
Parents said 'You can do anything'	Parents said 'Stand on your own two feet'	Parents said 'You're wonderful and brilliant at everything'
Kept opinions to themselves	Shared their opinions	Think you want to know their opinions

I could go on . . . but even from this brief summary, it's easy to see how disparity can happen. This highlights the need to be mindful of all generations and points of view, to treat people as individuals and for leaders to understand that the people they manage may well be very different from themselves. It's necessary to accept and embrace this rather than attempt to change what has been shaped from childhood by events, family and community.

One of our clients invested in a system to allow texts to be sent simultaneously to all (or some) of their workforce. This has significantly enhanced communication. People can opt out, but no one does. Everyone wants to be 'in the know' and since most text messages are read within 30 seconds of receipt it's far more effective than other more traditional methods of communication, although these should be also used as back-up and for those who prefer them. It's about thinking up better ways which fit in with today's 'multi-everything' workforce.

Generation Y is the first generation to have been raised in a truly digital age. They have grown up with mobile phones, internet and social networking, among many other developments. They know more, are younger, faster and therefore communicate in a different way from other generations. Generation Y say 'Why?' to meetings – why not Skype? As adolescents they consult their friends about every issue. Imagine asking your 789 'Facebook' friends whether you should dye your hair or not. This type of scenario has led to undeveloped problem-solving and decision-making skills. On the positive side, Generation Y people are very team-oriented and able to build relationships quickly. Because they do much of their socialising via the internet from the comfort of their own bedrooms, they'll also expect to be able to home work, flexibly.

I text my teenage girls when dinner is ready (really) because they are concentrating on their phones/homework/computer screens/music (probably all at once) and are inevitably wearing headphones. It's far less stressful than running upstairs and negotiating locked bedroom doors or shouting until I'm hoarse.

If we want Generation Y to hear, we must communicate in a different way.

My girls also tell me that Twitter is for 'old folks who don't know how to use Facebook properly!', so the best policy is never to assume and to find out how people like to receive information.

If you only do three things:

1 Be aware of how each different generation thinks and feels

2 Find the best (sometimes new) ways to communicate

3 Celebrate difference, get excited by the possibilities and make it work for you and your organisation

21

Benefits that excite and enthuse

The word 'benefits' is boring: not many would argue with that. It doesn't do anything for excitement and as a result, many people don't seem to understand what it means, what they're actually entitled to or how to, er, benefit. Yet benefits are something which we have to offer in our organisations in order to attract and retain the top talent and beat the competition. They offer us another fantastic opportunity to gain those 'Big E' (engagement) points and enrich the culture of your place of work, as long as exciting benefits are the menu of the day.

Now I'm not talking about expected rewards like pay, pensions and holiday entitlement here. We believe if you get the top five things right, these become less of a priority (although obviously you'd have to keep them at a fair and reasonable level). In fact, when we conducted our research, pay appeared at number nine on the list of things people need in order to be engaged, productive and retained.

The top five (just to remind you)

1. Communication

2. Leadership

3. Clear career path

4. Learning and development

5. Shared values with employer

Where to start

This is something that should be led from the top – it is not just an 'HR initiative' as exciting benefits form a fundamental part of what you are as an organisation.

On the basis that people are individuals and should be treated as such, we'd recommend you look at some sort of flexible arrangement when it comes to benefits – one person might trade off WLB against pay, or development opportunities over a Christmas hamper. There are web-enabled systems to help manage this if you're a large enough organisation, but if you're not:

- Find out what sort of things would make a real difference to people's lives, make you a better place to work; stuff that people will really appreciate

- Work out what's feasible or, even better, task a group of employees to do this

- Get organised and deliver – consistently

- Continue communicating, openly and honestly

- Keep checking that benefits are working for all parties

> **Remember: it's much harder to take away than to give, so start simply and build as you go.**

Appropriateness

Just because you're into snowboarding, fast food or bringing your dog to work, it doesn't mean everyone who works with you will be too.

While it's important to think about the individual, it's also essential to make sure the benefits you offer don't offend or alienate anyone. You'll need to make sure that what you offer is in line with your organisation, not only culturally but in terms of a fit with your brand, products and services, field of work. Overall it's a tricky balance, but when it's done well it's a great thing.

Below are some ideas to get your creative juices flowing. They're split into high cost and low/no cost because, although not everyone can or would want to invest in a helter-skelter between floors as a novel, fun way of getting from A to B, everyone can learn from, or at least be inspired by, the big boys.

Benefits should:

- Help people to do what they do best

- Help them to be happy and healthy

- Provide some fun

- Be flexible

- Be creative and cool

- Be appropriate

- Be very visible

Expensive stuff that people love (real life examples):

- You'll have heard about on-site nurseries, but how about the American bank that has an on-site school to make life über-convenient for parents?

- And, yes, there are in-house gyms, but what about bowling lanes, a climbing wall, running track, bike path or swimming pool?

- In-house concierge

- Dry cleaning and laundry service

- Free on-site doctor, dentist, chiropodist, nutritionist, yoga teacher, counsellor

- Free meals and fully stocked fridges available all day, every day

- Hiring out Topshop/Lush/Nike and giving everyone an amount to spend

- Health spa, hairdresser, spray tan (really), beautician

- Subsidies on hybrid car purchases

- Meadows with goats that mow and fertilise the grass

- Games centre with Karaoke, Wii, Xbox, pool, table football

- Company trips to exotic locations

Steal the ideas – you may be able to deliver versions that require a lot less financial commitment.

 **Chapter 21**

Low-cost or no-cost ideas you could also put in place (real life example):

- Chill-out space/nice place to relax

- Writing up people's achievements and good feedback on walls

- In a multicultural workplace, a big map on the wall showing everyone's country of origin

- Murals produced by or about the employees and/or your culture/values

- Non-work-related e-learning opportunities

- Discounts negotiated with local providers

- Subsidised gym membership

- Fruit, healthy snacks and drinks, free tea, coffee

- Food and drinks during or after company or team meetings

- Company competition or challenge with decent prizes

- Having lunch together

- Ice cream on sunny days

- Pay someone to wash people's cars in the car park

- Wi-Fi and internet available for personal use away from work area

- TV to watch World Cup, Olympics, royal weddings

- Day off to do charitable work

- In-chair work massage

Benefits that excite and enthuse

- Work station assessment

- Experiences that will benefit individuals and teams

- Matching funds raised via charity initiatives

- Use of facilities offered by companies or discounts (added benefit to the organisation of product knowledge and feedback)

- Allowing people to decorate own work space

- Random thank yous like gig tickets, vouchers, a relevant book

- Handwritten notes and thank you cards

- Birthday cards and celebrations – it only takes a little organisation and effort to have cake

- Holiday on your birthday

- Baby Gap vouchers for new parents

- Mentoring, buddying and coaches

- Trade for services board (people can offer their talents to colleagues on a reciprocal basis – 'I'll decorate your bathroom if you set up my home IT')

- An extra day off for a job done exceptionally well ('Get out of work free' cards)

- Team drinks on a Friday

- Company run/sporting event

- Team picnic

- Fun budget – allocate a small monthly budget for cool stuff to do together

- Awards, wall of fame

- Using employees in marketing materials and TV ads

- Movie nights, theatre

- In-house library

- Connecting people with others to help their careers

- Scrapbooks to mark milestones, special edition of company newsletter

- Home working

- Sabbaticals

- Allowing music and/or earphones at work

- Graffiti/self-expression wall

- Allowing some holiday time to be taken in two-hour blocks

- Interest-free travel loan (not creative but it can make life a lot easier)

- Anything that will benefit families as well as the individual

- Allocated time, without question, to work on non-core projects and innovations

You'll love some of the above and hate others – which is where appropriateness comes in. Think about them – there's always something you could do or do better ...

If you only do three things:

1 Consult your people

2 Introduce at least one visible, exciting benefit that really reflects your culture

3 Be consistent and communicate well

22

The departure lounge

Some people are going to leave you and actually that's healthy. If you can get to a stage where there are never any surprises because you are communicating and planning for the future with all your people, that's a job well done. We'd feel there was something very wrong at learnpurple if anyone handed in his or her resignation letter out of the blue.

Obvious truth

The key to retaining people is to create an environment and circumstances whereby they won't want to leave.

Everyone who is responsible for supervising another must understand the enlightened way to manage for the future. It's not difficult; it just requires a little technique and a lot of follow through. Right from interview and selection stage leaders, managers and supervisors should be asking, 'What's next?' Though not in a way that sounds as though you want people to move on.

'We hope you'll stay and grow with us: however, if you feel you'd like to try something new, please talk to me about it as we'd like to help you to reach your potential and it will help us plan for the future.'

Most people don't know what's next for them, so the ideal scenario is to:

- Regularly review progress, development needs, goals and aspirations

- Frequently ask the question, 'What's next for you?'

- Coach people towards clarifying and achieving their goals

- Help each individual work towards their life goals as well as their work goals

- Very important: realise that not everyone wants to stay for ever, so make the most of their time with you. This is the one managers find most difficult – it's a fact of life and the

big (not-so-secret) secret is that if you take this approach people are actually more likely to stay with you longer. This is because:

○ They feel under no pressure to stay

○ They know it's healthy and accepted for people to move on

○ They know they'll be supported and developed towards this

○ They know they can talk about how they really feel and where they're headed

○ They're less likely to defect to the competition out of loyalty for you; the enlightened and reasonable employer who will help them get what they want

○ You'll score Big E points galore

○ And if you know what to expect, chances are you'll be able to find them an opportunity within or outside the organisation that will suit both parties

If you're breathing a huge sigh of relief when someone hands in their notice, there should have been firmer performance management and guidance (see Chapter 12) before then.

Sometimes people leave because they don't think the organisation will be able to accommodate their requests. We're firm advocates of working round the challenge. Someone may have a burning desire to rediscover their inner self atop a Tibetan mountain or to return to Australia for a month. They may be ill and unable to travel into the office or need time off to care for a relative. Trade off the downsides of providing a sabbatical, work break or home working for a while and keeping your well-trained and knowledge-rich employee against starting all over again.

If you're creative and willing to work round people's challenges and needs, there's almost always a way to find a compromise and retain valuable talent.

This is not about being a 'soft touch' – it's a sensible, business-savvy way of thinking. Loyalty breeds loyalty and making an effort to support and accommodate people always pays off in the longer term.

Sometimes people go as far as they can and, especially in smaller businesses, feel they need a new challenge. It may be that you can provide this by way of a project, secondment, new assignment or by providing some development. If not, and they really have to go, help them find their new role, make their departure easy, supported and enjoyable. You might want them to return one day; they'll certainly tell everyone what a great employer you are if you treat them with respect. I need not remind you that this is not a divorce, so it shouldn't come with the same trauma!

When people leave

Being positive about leavers is very important for those who are left behind. They want to be able to feel they can maintain personal relationships without letting the organisation down.

Write leavers a great letter to thank them for their hard work and the contribution they've made.

If you want to 'leave the door open', do so very obviously. People might not return, but they'll certainly recommend you to others as a great place to work.

Give people a legendary send-off. At learnpurple we've done special spoof editions of our newsletter, fab leaving parties with poems and celebrations. And a photo album or scrapbook of their journey with you is a lovely thing to do too. At the very least you could buy a card and get everyone to sign it.

Pay promptly and accurately, producing the necessary documentation without delay.

Learn as much as you can about why the person is leaving and where they're going – this is a valuable opportunity to make improvements or to manage any misconceptions (though really you should have picked up on these before this point).

Chapter 22

Exit interviews

This is when a leaver is asked a number of questions about things like:

- Reasons for leaving

- Where next?

- Knowledge transfer/handover

- Recruitment and induction

- Comments on culture and values

- Systems and processes – what works and what doesn't

- Development

- Progress

- Leadership and teams

- Opportunities for improvement

In an ideal world every leaver would have a positive one-to-one exit interview. For tools and techniques, see the interview guidelines in Chapter 5.

In the real world this rarely happens because of time constraints – it falls to the bottom of the list of priorities and is almost impossible to keep track of. Often if exit interviews do happen, little, if anything, is done with the outcomes.

We'd therefore recommend automating this process to make sure it happens consistently – an online system can always be supplemented with face-to-face meetings if desired. And an online system will automatically collate outcomes so that useful data is produced and can be used to best effect.

If you do only three things:

1 Be brave – keep helping people working towards their potential even if this means they might eventually have to move on

2 Manage round issues to keep good people

3 Say thank you, provide a great send-off and find out as much as you can

23

What you need to do next:
how to achieve maximum
value from *Purple Your
People*

The trouble with business books is that when you're reading them you're inspired, have loads of great ideas and even greater intentions. Then you close the book, get back into the day-to-day running of your business and nothing really changes at all.

You're a bit more knowledgeable, so when someone says 'Have you read . . .?' you can nod.

You can pull out the odd gem at appropriate times and use it.

But it's not really changed your life or your organisation for the better.

Yet that is exactly what we want this book to do for you – change; transform even.

It's a bit like consultants. They come along with their heavy briefcases, asking you and your people a lot of questions. They compile a comprehensive report telling you what you should do, and the good ones even tell you how. But then they go away and you're left to sort it out yourself.

Business books are a gift to people like us who can steal ideas and share them, helping people to implement them; and we hope that this will happen with our book. But if you're the brave and busy person running an organisation or part of one, or heading up a team, we want to dedicate this chapter to you.

Before you relegate your copy of *Purple Your People* to the bookshelf, please spend some time planning what you're going to do next.

1. Make sure everyone in your organisation with any sort of supervisory, management or leadership responsibility, and those aspiring to reach these heights, reads this book. **Only by making sure that people understand the 'whys' and 'what's in it for them' can you begin to gather commitment to change.** If that's too scary, as a starting point make sure your leadership team reads it. Then work towards a situation where anyone could read it and you know they'll be able to say, 'Oh yes, we do that already.'

2. The wheel below represents the 12 key areas of the 'Purple Plan' covered in this book:

1. Reputation and market awareness

2. Culture/DNA

3. Attraction

4. Selection

5. Pre-joining

6. Induction

7. Performance and talent review

8. Goal alignment

9. Leadership, team dynamics and ASK (attitudes; skills; knowledge)

10. Risk analysis, succession and aspirations

11. Communication and opinion

12. Exit and follow up

Right now take a pencil and score your organisation against each one. The spokes of the wheel represent a 0–10 scale with 0 in the centre and 10 on the outer edge. Mark a cross at the point on each spoke to indicate how well you think you're performing in each area.

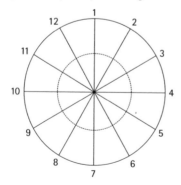

So for market reputation for example: if you think you're known as a terrible employer, notorious for poor practices and a high labour turnover, that will earn you a 1. Or you might be a recognised great place to work with on-spec job applications flocking in at the rate of 50,000 per year. That earns you a 9 or 10. Chances are, you'll be somewhere in between.

> We believe the most important thing to tackle first is culture/ DNA – your values and 'how we do things around here'. This is because everything else flows from this. You might already have a strong culture and values and know where you're heading. But does every single individual know, love and deliver on those values and purpose?

Once you've rated all 12 spokes, join up the crosses so you'll end up with something like this:

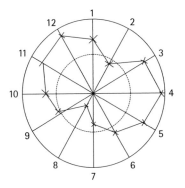

This will highlight strong areas and those requiring development.

3. Now think about which area is the most important for you to see an improvement – usually the one that will bring you the quickest returns and fix the biggest issues. Remember, this is all about business improvement – you're not doing it just to be nice.

4. Next, get your teams to complete the wheel – you can make this a fun session and get them to do it in groups, otherwise you'll be left with lots of bits of paper you won't have time to do anything with. You could even plan a company meeting or conference around this book.

5. If you're in a larger organisation where there's some resource to work on a master plan:

● Work out what you could do to improve each area and prioritise: the ratings on the spokes will help. Or call us and we'll come and help you

● Build this into a clear action plan in manageable chunks, using SMARTER goals, clearly allocating responsibility, defining metrics, review process and communication plans

● Decide who will have overall responsibility for driving this throughout the journey

● Do it!

All the plans in the world are worth nothing if you don't, in the words of Nike, 'Just Do it'. People spend far too much time deliberating instead of taking the first step and gathering momentum as they go. If you want to see poetry in motion when it comes to getting things done, take a look at Orient Express HRD, and friend of learnpurple, Sara Edwards. She 'just did it' in royal fashion with amazing results. And all from a simple one-page HR strategy:

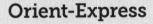

Orient-Express

Sara Edwards gets things done. When she joined Orient-Express in September 2009 as group HRD she quickly recognised that a global solution was required to bring connectivity and consistency to HR processes in each organisational location.

After four days in the office, she whizzed off on a three-month trip around the globe. Glamorous as it may sound – visiting the likes of Peru, Myanmar and the Copacabana Palace – she was working non-stop. Building relationships at every level, getting to know each business, understanding the organisational culture, identifying business needs; and, incredibly, she met with all 8,000 employees in the 50 businesses under the Orient-Express collection. Sara believes that you cannot be a great HRD without understanding everything about your people, your organisation, its culture and vision.

On her return, she proposed to the board a large project focusing on leadership and improved HR. She felt it was critical to have the right leadership team at the top and in every business and so had to make tough decisions around weaker leaders so as not to damage the business. She also knew HR had to be aligned with the CEO and finance director (a holy trinity, she says), so she worked hard to bring them on board with her on this journey.

Sara knew what she had to do and how she had to do it and the result has been significant. Labour turnover had decreased by 2.5% over the previous year. Within 12 weeks after implementing her talent toolbox™ she saw a 95% completion rate of performance appraisals around the world, promoted those who may not have been spotted previously (in one location they made the corporate chef general manager after reviewing his appraisal), and an 85% response rate on the employee opinion survey, with a company average of 77%.

To continue with your action plan:

6. If you're in a smaller organisation and you're anything like we are, you'll have learned that the best way to get things done is to start out with an idea of where you want to get to and an overview of how you're going to get there and then dive in and build it as you go. So you could:

- Define your values and DNA. In theory this could take days and weeks, but it can be done in one day if you have a well-structured approach and are determined to get outcomes and defined behaviours. Bring in an expert – it's definitely worth it.

- Deliver some fun interactive sessions with your people to make sure they know, understand and love your values, how they'll know if they're delivering (or not) and what they need to do to get there.

- Take the next most important area and put some effort into that using the relevant chapters of this book.

- Keep it simple. None of this stuff is difficult or out of reach. It just needs a whole lot of determination, some time and effort.

- Communicate throughout.

- Measure what you're achieving to keep everyone motivated.

7. Keep measuring how you're doing against your wheel – fill it in regularly: you should be moving towards a wide, smooth shape. Other things you could measure to show how you're improving (any, some or all) are:

- Sales/turnover

- Profit (gross/net)

- Customer satisfaction feedback/mystery shopper results

- Repeat business

- Employee satisfaction/happy scale

- Labour turnover

- Absence levels

- Productivity

- Recognition – awards, external ratings

- Number of on-spec job applications

- Idea generation

Measure before, during and after each improvement. Get people measuring stuff themselves – it should never be a big surprise. In the words of Sean Wheeler, Group HRD at the delightful Dorchester Collection and probably the most organised and productive man we know, 'what gets measured gets done'.

At the end of the day, if you're close to your organisation, you'll know if things are getting better.

8. Keep this book close at hand so you can dip in and out whenever you need some hints and tips or a reminder of why it's so important. Turn the corners of the pages down, write in it, stick torn-up bits of Post-It in it – go on, we won't mind. This is a book to be used and exploited; we hope it will be the best £12.99 you've ever invested.

9. Visit www.purpleyourpeople.com and register your book using the code:

TRANSFORM ME

You'll then gain access to a wealth of free resources and videos which will help you in your mission. You'll also be able to join our Purple Revolution for free which will give you access to free stuff and we'll email useful bits and pieces to you regularly to help you have inspired, happy and more profitable people.

Bonus point: if there's anything you don't quite get or have some feedback, or want to talk about finding some help or guidance, you can email me at jane@learnpurple.com. Read our blogs at www.learnpurple.com/blog and follow me on Twitter@JaneSunley.

If you only do three things from this entire book:

1 Sort out the culture and values stuff

2 Make sure you have capable and inspiring leaders at all levels

3 Find a simple yet robust way to manage performance and aspirations – consistently

And one more thing . . . register your book at www.purpleyourpeople.com.

Good luck – we're really excited for you!

24

Fun stuff:
the weird and wonderful
colour purple

The first recorded use of the word 'purple' in English was in the year AD 975.

It's a secondary colour made up of blue and red; embodying the balance of red stimulation and blue calm.

Few, if any, words in the English language rhyme with the word 'purple'.

Connotations

Purple is the colour of passion, romance and sensitivity

Purple cow: something remarkable, eye-catching, unusual.

Purple prose: exaggeration, highly imaginative writing.

Purple patch: a period of outstanding achievement.

History

Egyptian queen Cleopatra loved purple. To obtain one ounce of Tyrian purple dye, her servants soaked 20,000 Purpura snails for 10 days.

Alexander the Great wore purple robes, as did Roman emperors.

Leonardo da Vinci believed that the power of meditation increases 10 times when done in a purple light, as in the purple light of stained glass.

Purple is associated with:

- ambition
- spirituality
- wisdom
- psychic awareness
- lushness
- business progress
- patronage
- dignity
- richness
- royalty
- mysticism
- power

In Elizabethan England, the law dictated which people could wear the colour purple.

Pop culture

Purple was the favourite colour of rock legend Jimi Hendrix, who wrote the iconic song 'Purple Haze'.

Richard Wagner composed his operas in a violet room, his colour of inspiration.

Purple is the favourite colour of Prince (who penned signature song 'Purple Rain') and Justin Bieber – both of whom encourage their fans to wear purple to their concerts.

Deep Purple are a legendary 1970s rock band.

In *Star Trek*, the Klingons have purple blood.

Sport

After almost 140 years of playing in white, in 2010 England's rugby team revealed a new purple change strip.

The purple pool ball is worth 10 points.

Irish cricketer Kevin O'Brien dyed his hair purple in 2011 before hitting the fastest ever Cricket World Cup century (against England).

The LA Lakers play in purple and gold.

Italian football team Fiorentina play in purple.

Purple is a popular racehorse name, e.g. Deep Purple, Purple Ronnie, Purple Land, Purple Moon.

Spirituality and healing

Purple is an inspiring and spiritual colour. It represents the highest chakra which is about enlightenment.

Chapter 24

Purple is considered by many to be a 'high vibration' colour, providing an ability for purification.

It is said to be effective to use when strong detoxifying of the body is needed.

Purple is believed to be purifying to the body and the highest stimulant for the nervous system. It is inspiring to the mind for restoring mental equilibrium.

Purple is said to help develop the imagination.

Purple is the colour of good judgment.

Purple represents intuition, mysticism, inspiration and creativity.

The colour purple featuring strongly in a dream symbolises personal transformation and spiritual growth.

Around the world

Among Native Americans purple denotes wisdom, gratitude, and healing.

In Asia purple signifies wealth.

In Thailand, a widow in mourning wears purple. Also in Thailand anyone may wear purple on Saturdays and anyone born on a Saturday may adopt purple as their colour.

Purple pigment was used in the decoration of China's Terracotta Army.

The Chinese name for the Forbidden City literally means 'purple forbidden city'.

Purple needlegrass is the state grass of California.

The purple frog is a species of amphibian discovered in India in 2003.

The Purple Rain Protest marched against apartheid in South Africa – police water cannon with purple dye sprayed thousands of demonstrators. This led to the slogan 'The purple shall govern'.

Purple at war

The Purple Heart is a US military decoration for soldiers wounded or killed in battle.

A Purple Alert is when the UK or US army, navy and air force are called to mobilise together.

Purple is an emblem of authority and rank.

Before and during World War II, the Japanese used a code known as Purple or the Purple Code.

Psychology

The colour purple is thought to symbolise mystery and therefore could represent, in psychological terms, deep intuition or awareness of some as yet unexplored dimension of the self.

The rare condition whereby people fear the colour purple is known as porphyrophobia.

In the garden

As red roses symbolise the emotion of love, the purple rose stands for love at first sight. Dark purple roses symbolise deep-rooted and close relationships.

Cherokee Purple is a heritage tomato variety.

Asparagus comes in purple as well as green and white.

Chapter 24

Really, though, we became purple just because we like it!

> learnpurple's head office in London's Covent Garden is known as the Purple Palace and our people are the Purple People. We have purple values, a purple wall, purple stationery and even purple Christmas trees, as well as many other purple things!

Live your brand through your people!